Michelle
Have an
Extraordinary
Life!
Joy

How an Ordinary Woman

Can Have an Extraordinary Life

The Formula for the Art of Living Well!

Joy Weston

St. George Press
Westport, Connecticut

First printing 2002

ISBN 0-9716354-0-4

LCCN 2002100924

ATTENTION CORPORATIONS, UNIVERSITIES, COLLEGES, AND PROFESSIONAL ORGANIZATIONS: Quantity discounts are available on bulk purchases of this book for educational, gift purposes, or as premiums for increasing magazine subscriptions or renewals. Special books or book excerpts can also be created to fit specific needs. For information, please contact St. George Press, PO Box 2508, Westport, CT 06880, phone 203-222-7197.

TABLE OF CONTENTS

Table of Contents

This book is dedicated to the ones I love who have helped turn my ordinary life into an &xtraordinary one. Thank you so much, I couldn't have done it without you.

ACKNOWLEDGMENTS

Producing a book is a very interesting process, and far more difficult and arduous than most of you can imagine. It certainly took a lot more than I expected, and that's probably why the Acknowledgments are always in the very beginning of the book. Because without all the assistance and help one needs and gets in order to bring their baby to birth, it probably would never happen! So with that in mind, I would now like to introduce you to my wonderful support system and share with them my deeply felt appreciation.

First and foremost is my adored husband George. It was his idea for me to write a book, and it was his never-ending, unlimited support that brought it to this place. If I had the pages of an entire book, it wouldn't be enough to tell him and the world, how indebted I am for his love and encouragement. Thanks Babe.

My dear friend Gerri Eckert who began the editing process for me when at best my writing was "interesting", and for contributing her Ah-Ha moment to the book. I will always be grateful to you for encouraging me and not damping my spirits so that I could finally get a manuscript worthy of Donna Risolo's expert eyes. Donna your thoughts and ideas were always right on, and without your help I am not sure anyone could have actually read this book! Shannan Humsjo, I can't tell you how much it means to a writer to get her manuscript edited with "love notes." It was so important to know that someone besides myself really loved and appreciated my book. Jennifer Gallace, when you stayed up till 2am just to make sure nothing had been missed my heart was touched. Thank you my ladies, all your efforts made such a difference.

Writing and getting your book edited properly is obviously very important, but without the right marketing plan your family are the only ones reading your book. With that in mind, there aren't enough words to express my gratitude and appreciation for my incredible assistant Ana Velazquez tireless efforts. Eric Gershman for taking me under his wing, and for Marilyn Millers wisdom and direction. The roller coaster ride to success wouldn't have been quite as smooth or half the fun without you. I am a blessed woman.

Good editing and a brilliant marketing plan are absolutely necessary to bring a book forth. But this book would have no content if it wasn't for "the girls." Thank you all so very much for being in my life and playing such an important part in making this book and my life such a success. You are the best! Now in alphabetical order…Thank you dear friend Marisya Brzyski, Emily Canelo, Cynthia Cariseo, Joelle Delbourgo, Cate Fering, Laura Gabriel Polanca, Ginny Hill, MJ Kemp, Dale Krenza, Joanne Kruger, Randi Lenahan, Suzanne Moffet, Sandy Mozenter, Carmen Pino, Kim Risolo, Diane Romo, Sheila Tronn, Diana Vytell, Nancy White and Ketsy Saffer the greatest Mom and role model of them all!

To my firstborn child and love of my life, Larry. My wonderful son-in-law Bob and my adored grandson Alex. My cherished brother H.M., and my dad Clinton Saffer, who continues to protect and guide me from above. Thank you so much for being the male energy that has always held me in esteem and made me believe in who I am and what I could do.

Last but not least, a very special thanks to my best friend and daughter Lindsay and my precious "superstar to be" granddaughter Mia. You were always my inspiration for showing younger women how to have an easier and more joyful life. Fabulous women who could benefit by using *The Formula For The Art of Living Well* as their handbook for having the *E*xtraordinary life all women deserve. I am always filled with love and appreciation for having the gift of you in my life.

Opening Thoughts

"Who is this person and what are her qualifications for writing this book?" is usually the question that pops into my mind when I picked up a book that seems to promise something. I thought you might feel the same way, so with that in mind I would like to introduce myself to you. My name is Joy Weston, and I am just an ordinary woman with ordinary thoughts and ordinary gifts, who for years has done a lot of pretty ordinary things. Like growing up in the suburbs of Philadelphia, going to school, falling in and out of love about a dozen times and eventually getting married and having a couple of fabulous kids. I've worked at various creative careers, traveled a lot and forever seem to be in the process of learning yet another one of life's lesson. I'm just an ordinary woman who has discovered the secret of how to have an &xtraordinary life, who now wants to share that secret with you!

When I stopped to analyze what had prompted me to create my own personal formula for the art of living well , I realized that much of my motivation for change was fueled by my desire to finally rid myself of my insecurities and to unravel the various lies I had turned into my self-destructive negative truths. The biggest one being that to have an &xtraordinary life you needed to be &xtraordinary! You needed to be bigger and better, with more money, better credentials, a better body and a more beautiful face, and simply put, a *better, more improved* version of who you were. I truly believed that if you had all or at least most of these bases covered, how could you *not* have a fabulous life?

Well apparently there must be lots of other reasons *not to* have a fabulous life, or all the beautiful, rich and famous people wouldn't be spending so much time and money with their doctors and therapists, or finding comfort in Prozac, pizza and pints of Haagen Daz ice cream!

If the process of getting older has taught me anything, it is that life can be difficult and dreams can be fragile. Trying to hold on during this roller-coaster ride called life was sometimes more than I thought I could handle. I constantly felt as if I needed to find different ways to stay strong and mentally fit just so I could stay on the course of who I was and where I wanted to be. This realization came to me long before I knew how or what to do about it. But what I did inherently know was that there was an easier and more joyful way to live life, and that if I could just find the answers, I could live that kind of life as well.

During all the years that I was on my "search and seize mission" for tips on how I could possible improve my life, I was also slowly changing the way I had been thinking. One of the biggest influences in my transformation was a very special man called Anwar Sadat. Mr. Sadat was a Middle Eastern leader whose life work was to change the prejudices of the world. He believed that if it was possible for *just one other* ordinary person to have an *Extraordinary* life, then anyone could have one. All you have to do is to simply study the person's way of thinking and acting and then adapt their ways to fit into your way of life. *Act as if* until these traits become a part of you. He believed that there are no &xtraordinary people, just ordinary people who are &xtraordinary thinkers!

So are you ready for the number one secret I have learned for how an ordinary woman can have an &xtraordinary life? It's the same way an &xtraordinary woman can have a pretty ordinary life. It's all comes down to perception. It begins and ends with a thought. How you choose to think, speak, act and react to the various events in your life, and whether or not you believe that you deserve to have an &xtraordinary life is how you create either Heaven or hell on earth.

How An Ordinary Woman Can Have an &xtraordinary Life; The Formula For The Art of Living Well, is my personal collection of stories and tips that I have been gathering over the years. Stories with a message, that through their inspiration and wisdom gently remind you that creating an &xtraordinary life is always created first in your mind with a thought. Something we all intuitively know, but too often tend to forget.

These are true stories, moments of epiphany that actually happened to either me or one of my friends. Women who aren't superstars or celebrities or worthy topics for the tabloids, just ordinary women who are living examples of how having an &xtraordinary life has nothing to do with wealth, beauty, or your occupation. Just ordinary women who have learned that having an &xtraordinary life is all about your frame of mind.

This book is designed to give you the inspiration, encouragement and tools necessary for transforming potential negative problem into a positive solution. Once you look up the issue that you are interested in and read the story, you will be able to understand and utilize the power you have over most situations.

Each story is followed by a page of tips to help you accelerate your personal growth and support the changes you might want to initiate. I have also put a set of duplicate Tips pages in the back of the book for you to use as a quick reference for reinforcement, or to be cut out and put wherever you might want as a source of support.

The message of this book is about being able to change a negative thought or action into a positive one almost as it's happening. It's about having and using the tools that will help you make sure that nothing will ever really rock your boat or destroy your inherent happiness for very long. Stories that help you understand that having an *Extraordinary* life isn't about what you have or what you've done, but how you choose to think, speak, act and believe about all the various circumstances of you life.

It's dedicated to women of all ages who within any normal week are living their ordinary lives. With dishes to wash, beds to make, dinners to cook, jobs to go to, as well as endless responsibilities and decisions that have to be made. Women who know that every day is up for grabs and every moment presents itself with another opportunity to check-in and see "who you are, what you want, and what you are doing about it." Women who have learned that having an *Extraordinary* life, or not, is really all about your attitude.

These cherished stories have helped to mold and change my life forever in the very best of ways, as well as for all the women who I have shared them with. And do you know what happened to the ordinary woman who learn how to have an *Extraordinary* life? She lived happily ever after!

With all my heart I hope this book does the same for you! En-JOY!

The Seven "Must Haves" for Turning an Ordinary Life Into an Extraordinary One!

1. **A sense of joy and happiness** about your life, even when things aren't going the way you would like. Knowing that every lesson is a gift for your growth.

2. **A sense of love** for yourself, others and the world you live in, can heal, transform, and create miracles you never ever thought possible. Love cures all.

3. **A sense of abundance** that has nothing to do with how much money or material possessions you have, but a knowing of your universal never ending supply.

4. **A sense of self-worth** that recognizes your true value and reinforces your own self-esteem. An unshakable respect and belief in who you are.

5. **A sense of good health** that starts with a mind-body-spirit connection and then carries through to a commitment to diet, exercise and heart work.

6. **A sense of gratitude** that never let's you forget how blessed you really are. An appreciation for all the gifts and assistance that never stops coming.

7. **A sense of making a difference** with your family and friends, associates and strangers. Living a life of doing thoughtful and random acts of kindness.

CHAPTER 1

Awareness

The Formula—Ordinary to Extraordinary!

In every person's life there is a moment in time when the clouds open up and the sun breaks through, and a brilliant light shines down on something that is so important to you, you can't imagine how you didn't see it sooner. Suddenly, everything becomes crystal clear and you now understand it all. My "moment of epiphany" actually took five years of "moments" to be realized. It all began in 1986 when I was living in New York City. I had gone to bed for the night when somewhere around 3:30 in the morning I woke up in a cold sweat. I had the most incredible dream, which was actually much more like a premonition.

I saw that in five years, somewhere around my forty-fifth birthday, three things were going to happen. One, I would meet and marry the man that I was going to spend the rest of my life with. Two, I would finally have some financial security, which was not always the case, since I was a single mom with two kids. And three, I would finally trust my own inner wisdom for all the answers I was always seeking.

As the days moved into weeks and the weeks moved into years, I told anyone and everyone who would listen about my premonition. Wherever I went whether it was to the video store, the corner deli, or the local café, if I saw a man who I thought was interesting, I would think to myself, "Could he be the one?" Eventually my friends started to treat me condescendingly, with little comments and looks that said,

"You have been talking about this for a very long time, don't you think it's time you got a life?" I even had my friend Nancy call me up on the phone and say to me,

"Joy, I am really worried about you. It's been four and a half years and you've told the entire world about this fantasy man you are going to meet and marry; meanwhile, you're not even seeing anyone you like!"

"Nancy, Nancy my dear friend, what do you think I am going to do? Jump out of my first floor apartment? Relax. I'll be fine. The worst thing that will happen is that it won't come true, and I will say, 'So much for premonitions!'

Even I could understand her concern; I was concerned too! My life had taken a nasty downward swing and it seemed as if nothing was going right for me. I had broken up with my boyfriend, and wasn't seeing anyone I would even consider being intimate with, and because of a drastic fall in the stock market my successful photography career had all but dried up, and my finances were in the pits. Things got so bad that one day I had to hide in my sleeping loft when the landlord came looking for his rent. Life was anything but *Extraordinary*!

On this one particular cold February night I had made myself some homemade vegetable soup, and had snuggled in with some magazines in front of the TV. I started to watch a movie called "Why Me?," and as the tears were rolling down my cheeks, I realized that my eyes had landed on an ad in the personals written by a man who I just knew was looking for me.

Finding the courage to answer this ad (something I swore I would never do) wasn't easy. Especially since at this time in my life I really was a damaged puppy. But if I have learned anything, it's that you must dig deep within yourself to find the strength to push into challenges, challenges that often teach you things about yourself that you never ever knew. So, I took the plunge and answered the ad, and the rest is history.

On my wedding day, as I was walking around basking in the love of my friends and family, I overheard someone say, "Can you believe she did it? She said she was going to meet and marry her special man in five years, and she really did it!" In that moment I got it. I really GOT IT! I got the last and the most important part of my premonition; I now trusted the belief that I have all the answers I could ever need deep within myself. In all the circumstances of my life, whether they were positive or negative, I had brought them into reality by using *THE FORMULA*. A specific A, B, C, D way of doing things that every single one of us uses everyday to create the positive and negative experiences of our lives; whether we realize it or not. A formula, that once fully understood and then utilized properly, can turn an ordinary woman's life into an *E*xtraordinary one!

Meeting and marrying my husband, who is really a terrific man—who also happens to be a successful, spiritually evolved man, certainly combined two of my long-held dreams. It can't be denied that having a partner who is supportive in more ways than one certainly can make life a lot easier. But life has proven to have too many twists and turns to hang your happiness on a man or momentary financial security. So marrying my husband isn't what changed my life. Everything changed when I really understood that it was my own thoughts and personal power that had created this relationship, as it was with most of the important events in my life.

By the Thoughts that you focus on…
The Words that you speak…
Your Actions and Reactions…
and whether or not you Believe
You Deserve to have what You Really Want….
Is how you create the experience called, Your Life.

Working backward from my wedding day, I saw that for five years I had barely *focused my thoughts* on anything else except bringing my premonition into reality. Every *action* and *reaction* was generated with this one *focused thought* in my mind. I *truly believed* that this premonition was a preview of the future I truly wanted and *believed I deserved* I would get. When I stopped to analyze other positive and negative events that had happened in my life, I realized that I had used the exact same process as *THE FORMULA* to create all the circumstances of my life.

Up until then I had credited all the good things that had ever happened to me to either good luck or some blessed coincidence. All the not-so-good things I blamed on lousy breaks, bad luck, or just plain bad choices. I had continuously credited my career successes and failures, my wins and my losses, even the quality of my relationships, to some force outside of myself.

Remembering *THE FORMULA* and its power has become one of my greatest tools in creating an &xtraordinary life. If there is something I really want or need, I check in to see how I am positively using *The Formula*. And if things aren't going the way I want, I look to see how I am using *The Formula* negatively. What thoughts am I focusing on? How am I speaking about this? What actions am I taking and how am I reacting? Most importantly, do I believe I deserve to have what I really want? Just observing, helps to remind me that the quality of my life and the people who are in it, all begin and end with my thoughts. Turning my ordinary life into an &xtraordinary one has become a game of "mind over matter." And darling, that's what it's all about.

Seven Tips for Becoming More Aware...

1. **Always be aware of what you are thinking.** The thoughts you focus on will create your life. Look at your life, and you'll know what you are thinking.

2. **Always be aware of what you are saying.** Your words are a reflection of what you are thinking. If they're not positive and supportive, change them.

3. **Always be aware that action reflects thought.** If you like or don't like the way you are acting or reacting...take a look at how you are thinking.

4. **Always be aware of how you believe.** If you believe you deserve to have what you really want, you'll eventually get it—if you don't—you won't.

5. **Always be aware that having an Extraordinary life**, begins with a thought and a commitment that comes from wanting the best life can offer you.

6. **Always be aware of your intentions** and let them be your guiding light. Intend to have the life you truly want and then be aware of what your intentions manifest.

7. **Always be aware of your choices.** The choices you make moment to moment create the threads that compose the tapestry of your life. Your choices will color your life.

CHAPTER 2

Forgiveness

The Gift of Seven Faults

"I want a great relationship…a loving, supportive, nourishing relationship with another human being. I want to finally find that special someone with whom I can share my joys, sorrows, dreams, and life. A relationship where we can be together but individually be everything we have ever wanted to be." If that's not the silent prayer of most women I know, the pot of gold at the end of the rainbow, the brass ring, the whole enchilada, I don't know what is!

I sure know that it's been true for me, because right or wrong, good or bad, one of the things that matters the most to me is being able to love someone and be loved in return. And because it is so difficult these days to find and connect with that special someone, once you do, it's even more important to figure out how to keep those embers burning long after the flames of passion have subsided. So, whenever I meet a new couple that seems to be blissfully happy together, I always ask them that burning question, "What is your secret? What do you know that the rest of us don't, and could you *please* tell me what I need to do to have some of that same good luck?"

When I was first married I had the good fortune of meeting a new friend for lunch who brought with her what I came to believe was the gift of a lifetime. She had arrived late for our date, full of apologies, explaining to me that she had gotten caught up in the search for the perfect present for her grandparents, who were about to celebrate their 65th wedding anniversary. "Wow!" I said, "65 years with the same person! Are they happy together?"

"Not only are they happy together," she said, "but they seldom ever fight and are still really in love." That was all I needed to hear to make "the question" come flying out of my mouth, "what is their secret?"

"Well," she began, "On the night my grandmother married my grandfather, she decided to give him as her wedding present *The Gift of Seven Faults*. She told him that she understood that he was only human and therefore he could possibly have a few faults. Because she loved him so much and wanted their life together to be filled with lots of love and joy, she decided to give him *The Gift of Seven Faults*. Whenever he would display any of these faults, she would agree to either overlook or forgive them. So as one year rolled into the next, whenever he did *anything* that had the potential of getting her upset or angry, she would make a conscious choice to include whatever it was he did, as one of his seven faults!"

My friend went on to say that she had once asked her grandmother how she could *not* get angry at some of the crazy things her grandfather did and not feel the urge to kill him? Her grandmother laughed and said that of course there had been hundreds of times when she had gotten angry, but she realized very early on that there really wasn't anything he could do (except murder or abuse her or one of her children) that would be worth destroying the loving relationship that they had created together.

Being fortunate enough to have a really strong loving relationship with a significant other isn't about finally finding the perfect soul mate, that one of a kind "dipped in gold" human being you have been waiting for your entire life. Relationships, just by the nature of bringing two entirely different people together who have invested a lifetime creating their own unique personalities and patterns of behavior, are not easy. It takes making a real commitment to the relationship and a willingness to do whatever it takes to make it work.

My friend went on to tell me that on those very rare occasions when her grandmother was really annoyed with her husband, and she was questioning her sanity in giving him such a gift, she would bring herself back to her real love by repeating this phrase to herself. "Even though you know that you are absolutely right and you can't stand the way he is behaving, is what he is doing really worth ruining the rest of your time together? If you get into a fight there will probably be some residual bad feelings even after you make up. Is it really worth it? If this were our last day together, would what he is doing really matter to me?" Almost always the answer was "No." And just like a diet, you can start a new every week and even lose a few pounds along the way, but to keep the weight off you need to keep on doing what you know worked in the first place. As my beautiful friend Cynthia always says, "Maintenance is the name of the game!"

Since the basic premise of having an *Extraordinary* life is that everything always begins with your thoughts and how you choose to perceive things, why not try giving someone you love *The Gift of Seven Faults?* Why not try and see if it would be possible to give some slack to this slightly flawed human being that you just happen to really care about and want in your life. Ask yourself the question, "In the scope of things, is this really worth the aggravation and fight it's going to cause?" And maybe, just maybe the next time you do something that someone else isn't particularly jazzed about, they will stop and remember your generosity of spirit and include your teeny-tiny flaw in *The Gift of Seven Faults* to you!

Seven Tips for Forgiving and Not Blaming...

1. **Stay centered in the here and now.** Stop the action, count to ten and give yourself the time and space to disconnect from your upset.

2. **Take responsibility for your own feelings.** They are caused by your beliefs and life experiences. Become response-able, not reactive to words.

3. **Look for the lessons in all your experiences.** What about this experience is familiar? What can you learn from it? What can you do for a different outcome?

4. **Look at the risk you are taking.** Every time you go into the "blame game" you take the risk of damaging your relationships. Is that what you want to do?

5. **Playing the blame game** only prevents you from seeing your part in the upset. It holds you back from moving forward to a place of forgiveness—let it go.

6. **Open your heart and mind.** When your heart and mind are closed, nothing positive can come in. Keep them open for love and forgiveness and see what happens.

7. **Be grateful.** Count to ten and remember all the reasons you are grateful to have this person in your life. It's hard to be angry while feeling grateful.

CHAPTER 3

Communication

As Easy as One-Two-Three

Ah, the differences between men and women. The mystery that has fascinated the minds of scholars and ordinary men and women alike. The source of endless books, magazine articles, and television shows. Yet nowhere do these differences rear their ugly head more than in the area of COMMUNICATION. He needs to be seen, heard and understood this way. She needs to be seen, heard, and understood that way. Neither of which is ever the same way, whatever that way may be! And that's only the beginning!

When my husband and I first got together, it didn't take us very long to realize that all the years we had spent developing our unique personalities had left its mark on how we wanted and needed to communicate. We knew that we loved each other and really wanted our relationship to work, but all our little bickering showed us that our *Communication* skills definitely needed some help. One day my husband arrived home from work very upset because a particular customer reneged on sending him a very large and long overdue check. As my husband went on to share his feelings of anger and disappointment, all I could hear was that someone had hurt someone I love very much. I immediately went into my "Little Miss Fix-It" reaction of "let me now tell you all the ways we can fix this and make you feel better."

Unfortunately, or fortunately as it turned out later, this was the *very last thing* my husband wanted to hear, and the worst thing I could have done! He went crazy. "Can't you understand that there are times when I just want to be heard and not fixed? All I want is a safe space to be able to share what's bothering me, without Dr. Joy coming to rescue me with her great advice! Forgive me, but I am not the least bit interested. It's not that your advice isn't worth listening to because, in most cases, it is. But right now I don't care how brilliant your words are I just want to say what I have to say and not hear a single word in response!"

How interesting...especially since I had often felt the same way, except I had called it "not being validated!" So many times I had told my husband about things that were upsetting me, like when he forgets the "us" in our relationship and I ache for more intimate talks and touching instead of being "Miss Fix-it," all I really wanted was to be heard. But he would go into his "Mr. Defensive Mode," and I would end up soothing his precious damaged ego! Since clearly this was not just a "George and Joy thing," we decided to tackle this problem together for all of mankind and ended up creating the world famous *One-Two-Three Solution*.

Here is how it works. Say you come home with something that's really bothering you, and you need to tell your partner about it without having to be concerned about their reactions, opinions, or advice. You say to them, "I have something to say to you and it's a *One*." A *One* says to the other person "I have something to say that is very important and I want you to hear me without any interruptions. These are just my feelings, and I don't want these feelings to be judged or for me to be made to feel wrong for having them. No disagreeing or agreeing, nodding of heads, rolling of the eyes, or smirking of the lips. Please, I need you to just receive this communication."

A *Two* isn't so dissimilar than a *One* except here a bit of input is OK, as long as the other person keeps in mind that it's input that is desired and not a full-fledge game plan of fix and attack. And a *Three* says "OK honey, do your thing! Here's your open invitation to "heal and minister." Any solutions or strategies that can add to, alter, or fix the situation are all welcomed and wanted!"

Learning and then practicing good COMMUNICA-TION skills with the people you really care about can turn your ordinary relationships into *E*xtraordinary ones. Knowing your worth and value to others, and knowing how and when to share your unique gifts, is acting from a place of wisdom rather than simply reacting out of habit. The *One-Two-Three Solution* really works! In fact it has become one of my favorite number games. So as they say, use it or abuse it: it's your count.

Seven Tips for Better Communication...

1. **Take responsibility for the other person's listening.** If you don't feel as if you are being understood, try again. Say it in a different way until you are heard.

2. **Take responsibility for what you've heard.** Don't be attached to the words or what you think they mean. Ask for clarity and repeat back your interpretation.

3. **Take responsibility for what you want to express** and what you want from the situation. Take a moment to be clear with your thoughts and then your words.

4. **Align your values and intentions with your actions.** When you live your life from your sense of integrity, you don't have to fear any honest communication.

5. **Listen to the silence as much as the words.** We learn as much about others from the topics people aren't willing to talk about, as from what they are.

6. **Be as open to the criticism as to the validation.** Oftentimes we learn more about ourselves and others from the criticisms, than from the compliments given.

7. **Be flexible and willing to re-think and re-group.** If in the middle of a discussion you realize your position has changed, be woman enough to say so.

CHAPTER 4

Self-Confidence

Always Play to the Audience That Applauds You

There's no denying it…life can be tough, and people can be cruel. Keeping your head held high, believing in who you are, what you are doing, and who you want to be, is often easier said than done. I have often thought that we/ourselves cause our own pain and suffering. Especially when we believe that we are above it all. So savvy and street-smart to the ways of the world, that we will be spared from having to experience the rejections and betrayals that so many others have had to endure.

It sure wasn't possible for my friend Mara, when her "perfect man/husband to be" decided after what she thought had been a glorious weekend together, that he no longer wanted to see her or continue with their relationship; "just because." Nor was it for my friend Louise who had spent endless hours trying to help her neurotic friend Sarena work through a rough time in her marriage, only to have Sarena ultimately tell her that "we can't possibly be friends any longer because we are so drastically different." Slice it any-way you want, even if the perpetrator is a self-centered, energy-draining, mean-spirited loser, when someone says that they "don't want you" in one form or another, it hurts.

Well after lengthy consideration, I have come to the conclusion that there is an antidote for the pain and it comes from within, in the form of a healthy dose of *SELF-CONFIDENCE*. *Self-Confidence* that indestructible magnetic field of true self-esteem, deflects all forms of vic-tim-like emotions so that your authentic self no longer feels the need to take *anything* personally. An unwavering sense of self that helps you to always trust and support your inner wisdom, as it helps you find your own personal power in handling all of those below-the-belt punches and ankle biting experiences, that we all seem forced to experience at one time or another.

My personal "Ah-ha" moment occurred at my photog-raphy studio in Philadelphia, where I specialized in creating moody black and white portraits that would express the essence of who the person really was. During the photo sessions I would often ask provocative questions just to loosen up the clients a bit, with the hopes that they would reveal just a little bit more of their true personalities to me and the camera. Many of the secrets they shared with me in that blackened room with the bright lights shining down on them, were not only revealing but often times quite in-spirational. One of my absolute favorite stories came from a most unlikely teacher of *Self-Confidence*, which is prob-ably why her story has so affected the way I now live my life.

Sylvia Walsh was a woman who totally fascinated me. She wasn't a great beauty, nor was she a leader in her field or a great intellectual, and she certainly wasn't one of my more famous celebrity clients. But what she did possess was the most incredible sense of her self. She had such a powerful presence, that without exchanging a single word, you just knew that this woman possessed an unshakeable belief in her own personal value and worth. The self-respect, admiration, and obvious love she had for herself filled the room, and it was intoxicating. The longer I focused my lens on her, the more intriguing this woman's aura of self-assurance and confidence became.

Finally, when I couldn't take the suspense any longer I said, "Sylvia, I have got to ask you something. I realize that you are a bit older than I am, so I am asking you this as one would ask a mentor or role model. What is your secret for developing such an aura of self-confidence and belief in your own self-worth?" With her head thrown back an a delightful laugh, she replied,

"Joy, I have to admit that I am one of the lucky ones. I had the most wonderful mother who realized early on that while she personally thought I was the best thing since chocolate pudding, I sure as heck wasn't ever going to be the next Miss America. So she taught me how to recognize and then develop my unique and personal gifts, as well as to never forget and to appreciate who and what I am. Then she gave me some advice that I believe has been the secret to my success.

When I was just a young woman going off to college, my mom took me aside one day and said, "Sweetheart, I want to tell you something. The world that you are living in these days can sometimes be a real tough place. And the people who are living in this world with you can be even tougher. For a hundred different reasons, people will hurt, reject, disappoint, and abuse you. Some will do it accidentally, others will do it intentionally. Your best defense is to never forget how special a person you really are, and to never waste your time or energy trying to convince someone to believe that or to think the way you do. If you can always remember to *Only Play To The Audience That Applauds You*, your life will be a lot easier and a lot more fun!"

As my friend Cate once said to me, "The greatest treasure we have to share in this lifetime is the true gifts we were born with. If you are honest with yourself, your heart will tell you what you are best at, and show you the way to use your gifts. Don't compare yourself to others or worry about how many other people have the same gifts. You are as unique as the gift you have to offer. Use your gifts and the powers that will support you in your quest to share them, and you and the world will be a lot richer for it!"

So the question is, what are your unique gifts? The ones that only you can bring to the world, in the ways only you can do? Take Sylvia's advice. If you don't know what your gifts are find them fast. There are plenty of people who want and need exactly what only you have to offer! And for all the people in your life who feel the need to belittle or limit you for whatever reason, remember that everyone comes into your life to help you grow.

That doesn't mean that they are meant to stay forever. This is your play and you are the producer, director, lead actor and head of casting and ticket sales. It is always your choice as to who gets to enjoy your performances, and who is no longer needed in your production. The courage to act accordingly will come, once you truly know and honor your true value and self-worth.

There is no denying it, life can be tough and people can be cruel and sometimes the disappointments can be overwhelming. But once you make the decision to *Only Play To The Audience That Applauds You*, with all of your

SELF-CONFIDENCE intact, you might be amazed and quite joyfully surprised at who starts showing up at your sell-out one-woman show!

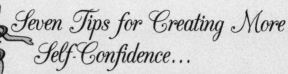

Seven Tips for Creating More Self-Confidence...

1. **Your level of self-confidence is up to you.** Change your perception of yourself and you will change your life. Choose to see your own magnificence.

2. **Be your own voice of self-affirmation.** Give yourself all of the compliments and acknowledgment you wish others had or could possibly give to you.

3. **Surround yourself with people who appreciate who you are.** Self-confidence is reinforced when others reflect your own glorious light right back to you.

4. **Give to yourself as you give unto others you love.** Be generous with respect and a deep caring for all that you are. It builds a strong self-confidence.

5. **Self-confidence is about trusting your own heart** and acknowledging your own personal wisdom. You know what's best for you because you are the best!

6. **Self-confidence comes from within.** Make working on your personal growth the most important thing, and you will learn to trust your own knowing self.

7. **Love yourself first and everything else falls into place.** Define the world in your own terms and then sit back and enjoy the accolades and applause.

CHAPTER 5

Suffering

How Important Is It?

It really doesn't matter how mature or evolved you may think you are, everyone has something or someone who really pushes their buttons. It might be things said about you, actions that were hurtful or diminishing, or a particular situation or experience that you just can't seem to let go of or get out of your head. Over and over again you replay the words that were used and what they really meant. Your actions and reactions and the disappointment and hurt you felt about the way things unfolded seem to dominate your thinking—until finally the time comes when you know enough is enough, and you need to get off it and move on. All your SUFFERING and struggle have become unbearable, and you ask yourself *How Important Is It?*

One day my dear friend Laura, who is an incredible spiritual minister, was sitting in the beautiful gardens of the local synagogue, waiting for Rabbi Gelberman to finish his lecture so that she could drive him home. When the Rabbi came looking for Laura he was upset to find her crying. He went over to her and said, "Laura, vat's vrong?"

"Oh Rabbi, I am so sad," Laura replied. "I applied to Weight Watchers to be an instructor and they turned me down. I am so disappointed because I really wanted that job."

"Laura," the Rabbi began, "do you know vat Shiva is?"

"Of course I do, Rabbi. It is the mourning period that you spend when you are grieving the passing of your mother or father, sister or brother, son or daughter, grandparents or a cherished aunt or uncle." Laura replied.

'That's right Laura. Now how much time do you spend in Shiva mourning the passing of a member of your family?" asked the Rabbi.

"Seven days, but why are you asking me these questions?" asked Laura.

"Because Laura," the Rabbi said, "if you spend vone veek mourning for your father or mother, sister or brother, son or daughter, husband or wife, grandparents or cherished aunt or uncle, how much time do you think Veight Vatchers is vorth? Maybe tventy minutes?"

Isn't that a great story to bring you back to reality and to really see how much time we waste *SUFFERING* over relatively unimportant things? Like everyone else at some point, you probably have spent way too much time and energy obsessing over something or someone who has done you wrong. Someone or something you will barely remember in five years, if at all.

Without any thought to the damage you are causing yourself, precious moments of happiness are being wasted in a no-win repetitive, punishing dialogue. That is set up by it's nature, to repeat the original punishment that this "someone or something" did to you, over and over again.

The next time you feel yourself falling down that tunnel marked "Hell: The Perfect Place To Obsess Over

Supposed Hurtful Things," stop and ask yourself, "Is this perceived problem, disappointment, rejection, or upset really worth all of the SUFFERING that I am going through? If in some religions we mourn the lost of our loved ones for seven days, in the big picture, *How Important Is It?*" If the honest answer is that this problem is really not worth such unhappiness and *suffering*, then pick yourself up, brush yourself off, and get back on the horse that is riding into the dance of life.

Turning our ordinary life into an *Extraordinary* one is as much about our moment-to-moment happiness, as it is about anything else. When you remember to ask yourself the question, *How Important Is It?*, you can begin to regain control of your emotions and improve the quality of your life. In that moment, and hopefully for many more, you can stop to remember what is really important in your life; like a healthy mind, body and spirit. And with a twinkle in your eye and a smile in your heart, you can stop and say to yourself, "Now really, is all the time and energy you are spending being upset and SUFFERING over what's going on really vorth it?"

Seven Tips for Letting Go of Suffering...

1. **Use your mind over the matter.** No matter what it looks or feels like, if you choose to think things will be better, sooner than later they will be.

2. **Learn to smile from the inside out**, smiling changes you mentally and physically. Put a smile on your face and the struggles hold a lot less power.

3. **Change your actions and reactions.** If you keep on doing the same things you'll keep on getting the same results. Positive actions get positive results.

4. **Think how you want to be.** Give up the struggle and suffering by seeing yourself as happy, successful living an abundant life. Fake it till you make it!

5. **If necessary, alter your world.** If where you are and the people in your life are bringing you down, change the people or change your viewpoint.

6. **Help others and you help yourself.** When you take the time to help others in need your problems seem to fade into the background. Caring feels good.

7. **Create your own support system.** Read magazine articles, books, listen to tapes, talk to friends. Find your own source of constant encouragement.

CHAPTER 6

Body Image

Accentuate the Positive and Eliminate the Negative

It's really amazing how obsessed women are with their body image. It doesn't matter if others see us as lean, trim, and perfectly curvaceous (or some other ideal image that this month's fashion magazines are trying to push): we all have our own "wish we could change and wish we didn't have" list. Unfortunately, when we look at ourselves the first thing our eyes often see are our perceived flaws. Daily phone calls, gym locker room chats and mealtime conversations are alive with discussions revolving around one's latest gripes and possible cures.

"I have got to go on a diet, I swear I can't fit into anything."

"So which one are you on, Weight Watchers, The Zone, Somers, Atkins eat-less-run-more or the cabbage soup, one raisin an hour plan?"

"Honestly I don't know whose body I am looking at; suddenly nothing is where it used to be."

"If my thighs, hips, stomach or butt get any bigger, fall any lower, or jiggle any more…"

"I am thinking of having some plastic surgery. What do you know about a tummy tuck, breast augmentation, liposuction, face lift, or belly button reversal?"

The conversations can go on forever and, minus a complete body overhaul or "youthifying" potion, what are we going to do? Is there a simple answer for having a healthy body image? Who knows, maybe it's as easy as singing a song.

When my first marriage broke up, my father had just died a month earlier and my life had totally flipped upside down and over again. Suddenly, nothing resembled the last thirteen years of the life I had known. In the beginning, I sure as heck didn't handle it very well. Since alcohol and drugs had never really been my thing, I turned to food for solace. I had never had a weight problem before, so when five pounds turn into ten all I said was, "Hmm, isn't that interesting." When ten went to twenty I thought, "Maybe I should start doing something about this." As twenty went to twenty-five and twenty-five went to thirty-five, I became so frustrated, all I did to help my cause was to eat in the closet so no one would know—ha, ha, what a joke that was! It wasn't until I reached a whooping forty-five pound weight gain, and found myself shopping in a store that only sold clothes for larger women, that I really understood what a problem I had. I went running from the store screaming for help, metaphorically speaking.

I had let myself go. Up until then the only time I had ever seen such weight on myself was when I was pregnant with my children. And when you're pregnant, the world embraces your "fatness" as natural and adorable. But it is quite a different story when all you can see when you look in the mirror is a size 6 wrapped up in a very un-adorable coat of blubber! And what made this even more pathetic is that at the same time that I wanted to hide out and not let anyone see me, I had one of my greatest fantasies come true: I became a national celebrity recognized for my photography. Suddenly, there were pictures of me everywhere I looked. On the television, in newspapers and magazines …little ol' me, and my forty-five pound blubber coat! And to mix everything up, I met a great guy who turned out to be one of my greatest teachers.

Daniel was exactly what I wanted at that time in my life. A bright handsome European, whose greatest desire was to love me and take me to Paris! Even though every day Daniel would make a point of telling me how beautiful and desirable he thought I was, I couldn't see it. All I ever dreamed about was showing him "the real me," not this secondhand fat version.

About a year and a half into our relationship, I finally got the courage to begin a health program of diet and exercise, and slowly but surely I began to lose the weight. I couldn't have been happier. My old clothes were beginning to fit again and I was beginning to like the face that was smiling back at me in the mirror.

I had so disliked the person I had become, changing myself into someone I could like again, became a bit of an obsession. So much so I didn't even notice the changes in Daniel's behavior. I remember one day when I was feeling especially proud of "the new me," I turned to Daniel and said, "Well, Sweetheart, what do you think? I look a lot better now, don't I?" I will never forget what happened next; in fact, it has affected the way I take care of myself and my body to this day.

He turned to me and said, "Well, since you are asking I will tell you the truth. I really don't think so. I actually preferred your more voluptuous body. I thought it was sexy and womanly and exactly how I prefer a woman to look. I always loved the way you dressed and carried yourself. To me you were like that wonderful American song …you always knew how to *Accentuate The Positive and Eliminate The Negative*. Frankly, it makes me quite sad to think that all this time you were hating yourself and not realizing how beautiful you really were!" Talk about a knife in the heart!

What I learned from Daniel that day and interestingly relearned again when I married my husband, is that beauty really is in the eyes of the beholder. There isn't one perfect body type for everybody. We all have our preferences and each of us has their own version of what we think perfection in that area is. Even though I have always craved cute little buns, all the men in my life felt quite the opposite. They love my curvaceous figure and beg me (can you imagine!) never to lose it. Hello Jennifer Lopez!

As my friend Joanne, a gorgeous woman who has been dealing with being a big woman for most of her life told me, "Being a woman who has lived a lifetime with a 'fuller body,' you would have to be a fool or a masochist if you didn't find a way to come to terms with what's really so with your body. And I believe that the same holds true for the woman who has gained a lot of weight because of some emotional, physical or life altering situation. Life is happening while you are living it, and it is up to you to make the best of it! Instead of focusing on the parts of you that you don't like, spend time improving the parts you do! Besides there is no such thing as one body type being the only good or desirable one. When a woman changes her attitude about herself by changing her opinion of her *BODY*

IMAGE, this self-acceptance and self-esteem are what be-gin to change the attitudes in our culture."

So there was the answer as simple as singing a song. "*Accentuate The Positive snd Eliminate The Negative, and don't mess with Mister in-between*" Why not choose to see your body through the eyes of someone who really likes it, in-stead of your judgmental critical ones? Focus on your assets and forget about those supposed flaws, and never forget that beauty is a very subjective thing! Maybe today is the day to try *Accentuating The Positive and Eliminating The Negative* and to remember there is no "supposed to be" perfect body. It's our differences that make us special and *E*xtraordinary.

When any of us forgets that and choose to believe the false myth that happiness and love will only come to those who are fortunate enough to have a certain shape or size, or a young tight body, we diminish our personal power and destroy our best cosmetic tool yet. An unwavering sense of your own unique magnificence, and a true appreciation for this body that has served you so well.

Seven Tips for a Better Body Image...

1. **Begin today practicing sweet talk.** Instead of telling yourself all the things that are wrong, try seeing and saying nice things to yourself.

2. **Beauty is in the eyes of the beholder.** No one size or shape pleases everyone. Try seeing your body through the eyes of the beholder who likes it.

3. **Look at the clothes you always feel good in.** Now repeat them in every possible combination. Accentuate the positive and eliminate the negative.

4. **Concentrate on the area above the neck.** Put a smile on your face, a twinkle in your eye and add an interested and interesting mind—they'll love ya!

5. **Your body is your temple**...take good care of it. Respect it—mentally, physically, emotionally and spiritually. Worship yourself; You're worth it.

6. **Create your own program for good health.** No matter what you've got—without your health—you've got nothing. Make it an important priority.

7. **Learn to be "bien dans sa peau,"** comfortable in your own skin. When others see that you are okay with your body, they will respond accordingly.

CHAPTER 7

Anger

If Not Now, When?

It's amazing how many different emotions human beings are capable of activating within nanoseconds. One
minute you can be feeling a great love for someone, and in
the next moment a great hate, or at least a great not liking
at all! You can be having quite a pleasant time, when a few
words are spoken or something is done, and suddenly your
joy turns into disgust. In seconds, someone you know and
love has turned into a two-headed monster, saying and doing
things that make you wonder *who is this person and why am
I with them?* Your great love has been replaced by a total
stranger who may look similar to someone you love, but
the resemblance stops there.

Unfortunately I haven't yet discovered any secret formula to truly prevent these uncontrollable erupting of
emotions or the spilling out of hurtful insensitive words
that often turn into fights. I certainly have read enough
books that expound upon the ways and means to having a
more saintly behavior; however I've discovered that saint-
hood is clearly not my calling. But what I can do is remember

a pearl of wisdom that my mother once told me. Wisdom that has helped to keep my marriage strong and loving with a minimal amount of detectable scars.

When I was a young woman and just beginning to really understand the dynamics between a man and a woman, it would always amaze me that my mother could be so mad at my dad one moment, and then just minutes later, act as if nothing had happened. One day after one of their disagreements I remember asking her how she could even be speaking to dad, no less acting as if nothing has happened, when just minutes before she sounded as if she wanted to kill him She looked at me with the eyes of a mother who was about to share with her daughter one of those invaluable life-changing lessons.

She began, "You know Joy, there will be plenty of times in your life when you will get upset with someone you love. It may be your husband, a girlfriend, a boyfriend, a parent, or a child. People just seem to get other people upset for a thousand different reasons, and unfortunately, angry words and gestures seem to come out. You're angry that they did this and they're angry you did that, and no one wants to admit that they are wrong. Each one has their own position and that's that.

The burning question is: for how long—a day, a week or a month—are you willing to stay angry at this person who you love or really care for? If you know that in your heart you don't really want to end this relationship, and that sooner or later you are going to make up anyway, the question is, *If Not Now, When?*"

Mom taught me that life is too precious and time is too short to waste it on "being right." There are no gold stars given out for the person who stays angry the longest. The only thing you'll get from that kind of behavior is heart-burn and aggravation!

So now whenever I get upset with someone I really care about, I try to remember my mother's words and remove myself from the line of fire. I usually go somewhere else to calm down for a bit, and then do anything I can to change my thoughts and refocus. I've even resorted to cleaning! After a while I am usually ready to say, "OK, time to let it go Joy. You know that you are *eventually* going to make up, so *If Not Now, When?*"

Saying the words *If Not Now, When*, always brings me back to the love I have for that person. It gives me the power to change my attitude and the strength to return to my commitment. It also helps me to look at the cause and effect of this *ANGER* and what it's doing to me and my day. This simple phrase enables me to return to "the scene of the crime," with a new conversation as if nothing has happened.

"I just saw the most beautiful birds on the porch. How unusual for this time of year." Since no one really wants to fight, the olive branch of peace in these simple words is usually enough to get us back on track and into the space that creates loving relationships so we can begin anew.

Even though there are times you may choose not to remember, you do have the power to control and change your thoughts, words, and actions. It's not always easy and sometimes it takes enormous effort, but you can do it if you really want to. Remember your dream to have an *Extraor*-dinary life and then say to yourself, "It's time to just let go of the *ANGER*, because *If Not Now, When?*"

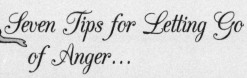

Seven Tips for Letting Go of Anger...

1. **Give up vomiting out hurtful words** based on problems or mistakes made in the past. Invisible hurtful scars remain long after the fight is over.

2. **Keep your arguing to yourselves.** Keep it private and don't involve outsiders. Don't gather judges in your defense or create gossip for later on.

3. **Stick to the subject.** Don't confuse the issue with things that can only diffuse the importance of what really matters. Stay with what's going on now.

4. **Don't throw threats into your fight** that you don't really want to carry out. This is dirty fighting and can cause serious backlash and added upsets.

5. **Keep it real.** Don't waste precious time hiding behind safe topics that prevent you from owning up to what's really bothering you. Honesty pays off.

6. **Steer your conversation towards finding a solution.** Speak to the other person's higher self. Help them understand with the intentions for this to be a win-win.

7. **Be a gracious winner**—remember, in a relationship there's no such thing as neutral—you either build it up or destroy it through your actions.

CHAPTER 8

Aging

Choose the Rain

I've thought and I've thought, and you know I can't remember a time in my life when aging wasn't an issue. *Forever* I have been "too young" to do this, or "too old" to do that. "No, you can't go where your brother is going; you're too young, and you're old enough to know that."

"Don't you think you are too young to go to a place like that, dressed like that?" Or, "Aren't you a bit old to be going to a place like that, dressed like that?" For years when it came to work, I was told I just didn't have enough experience, then suddenly, I was over-qualified! Then there is my all time favorite, *act your age!* Which after all these years I still haven't quite figured out what that's supposed to mean.

So now I have become "a woman of a certain age," which as far as I know I have always been *of a certain age*, except now it seems that this is something that I should be concerned about. Everywhere you look there are hundreds of books, magazine articles, and television shows intent on making sure that you're not living blissfully in some "eternal youth fantasy," as they remind you of all the potential problems that are lurking in every corner just waiting to get you as each precious moment is ticking by. Then they go on to discuss the perfect vitamins, foods and exercise programs that will guarantee that you will live a longer and better life, as you are waiting for the other shoe to fall!

As the saying goes, "I don't know if it's bad and I don't know if it's good," all I do know is that in the last two months I have been to four different gatherings with women between the ages of thirty and sixty-five, where at some point in the evening the discussion gets around to the problems of aging. Each one left me feeling depressed and hopeless, (especially since I have always felt that if God is really good to me, I will continue to get older!) It dawned on me that if I didn't find some way to truly embrace this *AGING* process and the inevitable changes that go with it, then I sure as heck was going to have a pretty lousy time over the next fifty years. And if it wasn't lousy, it certainly would be a far cry from being &Extraordinary!

So I went on a search to find some answers to aging youthfully with style and grace, which I found one sunny afternoon in New York City. I met my friend Sheila who happens to be a great advocate for "loving and honoring the exact age that you are fortunate enough to be." She told me a story about a date she recently had with a very attractive new man in her life, who at one point in the evening casually mentioned that he had graduated from high school ten years before she had. She said that suddenly she thought, "Oh my God, "that makes me ten years older than him. What if he thinks I am too old for him, and he doesn't want to go out with me? Just this one time I hope he doesn't ask me my age, because if he does, I don't know what I'll say!" And then this voice came into her head that said, "Sheila, *Choose The Rain.*"

She went on to tell me about a life-changing experience she had a few years ago with a very wise friend. They were having lunch together when she looked out the window and realized that it was raining cats and dogs. She started to complain about it. He listened to her for a moment or two and then said, "Sheila, *Choose The Rain.*"

"What are you talking about?" she replied with frustration in her voice. *"Choose The Rain, Choose the rain,* how can I *choose the rain?* I don't even have an umbrella!" With that he looked at her lovingly and replied, "Is the rain going to stop because you want it to? Is it going to just go away? Why not chose to see the beauty in the rain and let it add to your day instead of diminishing it?" In that moment, she understood exactly what he meant. If she chose to be happy with herself and the moment *exactly as it was,* as well as being grateful for all of the wondrous things that can come with the moment, her experience of life could be totally different and so much better.

So Sheila decided to *Choose The Rain* with this new man and speak her truth. "How wild, she said, I graduated exactly ten years earlier." With that the man looked at her with a smile and said,

"I never would have known it, but what a nice change to hear a woman mention her age as naturally as she would anything else. I guess I can understand why, but it seems so crazy that women actually think if they lie about their age or won't tell you what it is, it will really affect the way someone sees them. As I have gotten older I have come to realize, that youth and beauty are merely a state of mind. And in reality, age is nothing more that an interesting bit of trivia!"

Even though Sheila and her new fella only ended up being friends, his words were a gift she has shared with many of her friends. Now when I look in the mirror and my eyes insist on focusing on the latest wrinkle or the sagging *whatever*, I say to myself, "Joy, why not give up the flaw search and *Choose The Rain?*" With that thought in mind, I can refocus on the sparkle in my eyes and those adorable little laugh lines that are there *because* of all the years of enjoyment and blessings that life has given me. And when I get on that treadmill one more time, fighting gravity's cruel joke with all I've got, I can choose to acknowledge and be grateful for all the years this body has served me so well. In that one blissful moment I can proudly say, "this is what fifty-plus looks like!"

Years ago I read a quote from an interview given by the French actress Simone Signoret. Her philosophy is one I have since chosen to adopt as my own. She said, "When I die, I will be very, very young."

"Really, the reporter replied, and how young will that be?"

"Oh I don't know, maybe eight-five or ninety. But when I die, I will be very, very young!"

Seven Tips for Aging With Style...

1. **How you see yourself is more important** than how others see you. "Youthful" is a very personal thing. Age is truly just a number and a mind set.

2. **Don't buy into what others say is appropriate** for your age. Go where you want, do what you want, and dress the way you want. It's your life, enjoy it!

3. **See the changes in your appearance objectively,** not in the harsh light of age comparison. You just might discover a more beautiful and youthful you!

4. **Focus in on what is your best look** for this time of your life. Choose carefully and buy the best quality items you can afford. Make your own statement.

5. **Do things that make you feel beautiful.** Dress up or dress down. Laugh, sing, dance, go to parties, give parties. Do whatever, just do it with panache!

6. **Keeping your mind and body healthy and active** is vital for eternal youth. A fit body, sparkling eyes and an inquisitive mind are irresistible to everyone.

7. **Stay true to yourself and your own unique style.** The most beautiful women are the ones who don't submit to any standard of beauty. They define it.

CHAPTER 9

Happiness

Is a Way of Life, Not a Destiny

One of the things that has always fascinated me is exactly what information we tend to retain from *what* experiences and *why*. Why is it that I can remember the dress that Sue wore to Diane's party, but not where I went last week for dinner? And why in Heaven's name do I remember that bit of trivia, but half the time can't remember where I parked my car! I don't think I even want the answer to that one!

When I was probably around six or seven years old my family lived in an area of Philadelphia called Germantown. We often traveled down a very wide street called Lincoln drive, which among other things had two churches on it. The church that I remember the most seemed very big and white with a red door and a black board in the front. All the coming events were listed on this big black board in white letters, which I assume they changed every week.

On this one particular day my eyes were drawn to the black board like a magnet, as if I sensed that there was a message there that had been written especially for me. I must have been right, because I have never forgotten what

43

it said, nor have I ever stopped using it as the standard for the way I live my life.

"*HAPPINESS Is a Way Of Life, Not a Destiny!*" *Happiness is a way of life, not a destiny...* Wow, what a revolutionary idea! Magically I realized that being happy wasn't about whether I got the latest Barbie doll outfit, that cool red bike in Mr. Schultz's store window, or whether or not I was going to spend the summer at camp in Maine with my best friend Suzie. It was really about all of the moments lived in-between. Talk about having an Ah-ha moment! A moment in time that I truly believe has altered the way I live my life and has continually ignited the circuits of my highest potential for a better life.

In this materialistic world, you are often so anxious to finally "get to the good life," that you let life rush right past you. You spend so much time thinking about how great it's going to be once you get more money, move into your new house, find the perfect sweetheart or finally lose those annoying fifteen pounds. Then you get these things, and you know what? A lot of the times you feel as if something is missing. Strangely, you are not quite as happy as you thought you would be.

These magical elixirs that will solve all your woes, are often quite opposite of what you had hoped for. And to add to your disappointment, they come with their own set of problems. In the meantime life was just passing you by as you were deep in thought of what could possibly happen tomorrow. You missed another precious moment in time that will never come again.

HAPPINESS is a Way of Life, Not a Destiny reminds all of us to seek out life's little treasures that are hidden under or behind the remains of the day. They could be as simple as a hot bath on a cold night, getting the last slice of Mama's delicious carrot cake at the bakery, answering the phone and hearing the voice of someone you've missed. It could be catching a missed episode of your favorite TV show, getting a compliment from a stranger, or just the simple awareness of being alive on another glorious day! Remembering that *HAPPINESS is a Way of Life, Not a Destiny*, instantly brings you back to the present, and the knowledge of how much your moment to moment thoughts create the quality of your life.

Interestingly, I've noticed that the slightly older Joy hasn't changed very much over the years. I still get great pleasure from similar things that I wanted as a young girl; they're just slightly different. Instead of a new outfit for Barbie, I am more interested in a new outfit for Joy. And instead of a new red bike, I've got my eye on a hot new silver sports car I saw the other day. And instead of hoping to go to summer camp in Maine with Susie, I've been checking out air fares for a romantic trip to France with my honey.

And even though I am constantly updating my want and wish list, I always try really hard to keep my attention on the moment as I continue to hold my intentions for the future in the same space. Because of those nine wonderful words that I learned so many years ago, I am now capable of turning my ordinary life into an *E*xtraordinary simply by making sure I stop and take note of my daily blessings.

I have learned that postponing your *HAPPINESS* until "The Big Kahuna" comes rolling in, is a terrible waste of time. Appreciation for what you have right now is where it's at. Ever since I've learned that *HAPPINESS is a Way of Life, Not a Destiny*, I've made it my business to create my happiness, moment to moment. Because no matter what you think, this is really the only moment that you know for sure that you will have. Don't throw away another moment waiting for your fantasy ship to come in.

Seven Tips for Increasing Your Happiness...

1. **Allow yourself the gift of feeling worthy** and deserving enough to have all the happiness and joy that are a part of your natural birthright!

2. **Immerse yourself in the good times today.** Don't let the fears of the bad times take away from your potential happiness today—live in the moment!

3. **Fill yourself up with memories of happy times.** Let them be your strength and support to handle the many challenges that will come your way!

4. **Follow your bliss**—once a day do something that makes you feel happy and happy to be alive. Find your passions and then fully enjoy them!

5. **Do something worthwhile.** Experience being fully engaged in doing whatever gives you purpose and makes you feel worthwhile…and be happy!

6. **Make someone happy.** Do something special for a loved one, compliment a stranger, say a kind word. Their happiness will bounce right back at you!

7. **Choose to be happy,** choose to make happiness a constant part of your life, anyone can. It's as easy as saying "happiness is a constant part of my life!"

CHAPTER 10

Personal Growth

Focus on Your Growth

You think you're so cool. You think you've been around the block enough times to know where everything is and what's really going on. And then one day you're just going along minding your own business when you turn a corner and *bam*, you walk smack into a life-changing revelation! One of those V-8, light bulb, epiphany moments that changes how you see, hear, and do things for the rest of your life.

As a dear friend of mine once said, "You rarely learn your life lessons while shopping at Neiman Marcus." And even though this is really one of the best stores for anyone to shop their troubles away in, it usually takes being beaten to the ground by something that has brought you so much pain and suffering that you just can't take it anymore. It's an area of your life that *for whatever reason* you have chosen not to see or admit you needed to change, heal, or grow from. But now you can no longer avoid it. At that precise moment the universe says. "OK, I think this time she is finally ready to get the message."

Recently I had an experience with a woman that exacerbated one of my most vulnerable times. It happened at a period of my life when I believed that everyone and everything that everyone else had, was bigger, better and more wonderful than anything I could possible have. It was a time in my life when I sadly had forgotten who I was and my own worth.

It all began one summer when I befriended a woman who represented to me the world of the rich and famous. A special world that I had always dreamed of being in. Ah, the fantasies I had about being at all those oh so exciting parties, designer-dressed luncheons and spending time visiting their fabulous homes in wonderful places all around the world.

To me this life was like the beautifully gift-wrapped package at the very top of the closet, so bright and shiny, but always just out of reach. That *something* you have wanted for so long, that even after you opened the box and saw that what was inside was not at all what you had hoped it would be, you still *pretended* that it was everything you thought it would be. Often times this pretending comes at the great expense of lying to yourself about what's really going on. You surrender your own values, personal happiness and self-worth just so you can stay in the fantasy.

I wanted so much to be a part of the world this woman symbolized. *I pretended* that even when I heard her casually spoken, mean-spirited remarks about me (and everyone she knew) that it was only my silly sensitivity. *I pretended* her manipulative ways and conniving methods she used to get the things she wanted at all costs, were just her creative way of getting ahead. Even when she made it perfectly clear that she had no interest in my life, and my only value to her was to be a sounding board for her dysfunctional marriage, I still continued to *pretend* that this person was so much more a quality woman and friend than she was ever capable of being.

I saw a movie the other night that really brought this message home. It was about a single mom with four kids who really wanted a good man in her life. A man who had a decent job with some money in the bank, someone who would love her and her kids. She thought she had met such a man and her dreams had finally come true. And then one day she came home early from work to get ready for their date that night, and she found him already at her house, molesting her daughter in the back bedroom.

In the hospital, after being terribly beaten up by him for trying to defend her daughter, she turned to her friend and said, "The kids knew all along that he was no good, but all I could see was his shiny new Buick!"

In our lifetime each of us will get lots of opportunities to learn lessons that are necessary for our *PERSONAL GROWTH*. Often times those lessons will come with their share of pain, along with the aftermath of feelings of shame and disgust with ourselves for letting whatever it was happen. I know from personal experience that initially those feelings can't be avoided, "What was I doing? I should have known better. I feel like such a fool." But the sooner you can forgive yourself for being human, the sooner you can get back to living your life. I've learned that when you can *Focus On Your Growth—and not on the way you got there—* you can begin to move past the ego's cry for sympathy or revenge, and on to understanding the message behind another one of life's glorious learning lessons.

I can't tell you how many times I've thanked that woman for bursting my bubble. Because if she hadn't, I would probably still be trying to find my way to that elusive phony dream and denying my own personal Nirvana. As much as we might hate it, we usually only learn our big lessons when we are hit on the head so hard it hurts. Because of her "gift" to me, I am now capable of seeing my &xtraordinary life for what it is.

My life has become so much fuller and richer, and I can now see that fantasy and so many other illusions for what they really are. Now when I bring new friends into my life I look at the content not the wrapping, and I listen more carefully to the meaning behind any gold gilded words.

If I have learned anything, it's that any time you can forgive yourself for dancing with the devil and recognize the blessings that come from such experiences, you will have taken another step on the path towards your *PERSONAL GROWTH*. Using the light of your learning lessons to *Focus On Your Growth,* is one of the brightest way for any ordinary woman to have a truly &xtraordinary life!

Seven Tips for Encouraging Personal Growth...

1. **Free yourself from living by other people's rules.** This is your life. Do what you want with it and be consciously aware of the life you are creating.

2. **View every experience as a gift for your growth.** The best of times and the worst of times all help to create who you are and who you want to be!

3. **Judge less, forgive more, look for the best in all.** Everyone and everything has something positive to offer you. Find it and enlarge your heart and spirit!

4. **Ask, ask, and ask again for what it is you want.** Don't be afraid to ask people for what you want and need. Most people want to help you and will!

5. **Develop a passion for something you want to do.** Take risks and go for more than you think you can. Fear paralyzes and passion is fuel. Believe you can!

6. **Love with all your heart as much as you can.** Take pleasure, play and work seriously, and enjoy yourself. Be grateful for everything all day long!

7. **Live in the moment. Learn from the past. Let the future be designed through your intentions.** You are a master of creation—be open to the process!

CHAPTER 11

Gratitude

If You Only Say One Prayer

As corny as it may seem, I have always believed if there was just one thing you could do that would truly please The Source that created us all, it would be to fully enjoy the life you have been given. To express your GRATITUDE and your deeply felt appreciation for how lucky you are to be a spiritual being having this human experience. How fortunate you are for being given the free will to choose who you are and who you want to be, and where and how you want to live. And if you only had the time to say one prayer, let that prayer be *Thank You*.

Last week my husband and I went to dinner at the house of our friends, Jennifer and Bob. We had just returned from Italy and since they were taking a similar trip in a few months, we wanted to wet their appetites by sharing our pictures and stories. The dinner was great, the wine was flowing, and the laughter was light and gay. Then the phone rang. Almost instantly the energy changed as Jennifer and Bob gave each other a knowing look while they let the machine answer the call.

My friends have been dealing with a problem for quite a few years now that unfortunately has affected many families these days: they have a son who is addicted to drugs. A disease that drastically alters the quality of the life of the users, as well as the lives of their family and friends. And until you know someone who is caught up in this crazy dance you can't imagine how crippling and sad it can be.

But what's so amazing about Jennifer, is that if you weren't her close friend and didn't know the intimate details of the devastation that her son's disease has caused in her life, you would be enchanted by her upbeat personality. She is a joyful and loving woman who fully engages with other people and life, and I wanted to know how could she rise above this, day after day? What was her secret for turning those negative moments around, and turning her ordinary life into one that I considered quite *&*xtraordinary?

"GRATITUDE. *Gratitude* is the answer," she said. "Once I can get past the pain and upset of the situation, I make myself stop—wherever I am—and I begin to make a mental list of all my blessings. I begin with my health and the health of my family, then I move on to the roof over my head, the food on my table, and the clothes on my back. I think of my loving husband and all the good friends in our life, as well as all the abundance I have in my life. I thank God for the strength and support that I've been given to deal with my problems, and for all of the hundreds of memories I have for all the good times I have been fortunate enough to have. I've been doing this for so long, it only takes minutes for me to get centered after I am upset, and I always feel so much better afterward."

Making a mental note of your *Gratitude* can be just the soothing balm you need when life becomes too much to bear. It can also be the fuel that keeps the passion for life alive when things aren't going so well. I have never forgotten the words, *"If You Only Say One Prayer, Let It Be Thank You,"* and there is rarely a day that goes by when I am not chanting just that one prayer. I am always feeling so grateful for the *Ɛ*xtraordinary life that I am so blessed to be living. In fact I find myself repeating my prayer of thanks at what would seem the most unexpected times. I can be driving in the car, waiting for the deli man to slice my roast beef, or washing the dinner dishes. When either in my head or out-loud, depending on where I am, I find myself saying over and over and over again, *"Thank you God, Thank you God, Thank you God, Thank you God, Thank you God, Thank you God, Thank you God, Thank you God, Thank you God, Thank you God, Thank you God, Thank you God.*

And when I close my eyes and go to bed at night, after I mentally share my thoughts on the day and possibly ask for guidance or direction, I always repeat the same prayer. *"Thank you God for this day you have given me and the one that is coming tomorrow. And if you choose to give me no more, give me no less"*

When my husband tells me he's jealous that I always fall right off to sleep like a well-fed baby, I tell him that as soon as God hears my prayer of thanks the angels are instructed to kiss my eyelids so I can fall asleep and get ready to enjoy another *Ɛ*xtraordinary day!

Seven Tips for Having Gratitude...

1. **Having gratitude has a cleansing effect** on your mind, body and soul. Noting your blessings enlarges you from within and manifests magic outwardly.

2. **Showing gratitude by saying "Thank You"** all the time for everything, is a wonderful way to increase your awareness for things others take for granted.

3. **Having gratitude allows you to appreciate** your personal wisdom and power, and the gifts the universe is always bringing you through all of life's lessons.

4. **Having gratitude** can alter your energy and make you feel really happy just to be alive, allowing you to experience nothing less than Heaven on earth.

5. **Having gratitude helps you remember** that even in the eye of a storm God has put a rainbow in the clouds. You are blessed and being taken care of.

6. **Having a gratitude attitude changes the world.** A kind thoughtful word goes a long way in opening the hearts, arms and gratitude of others.

7. **Having gratitude can turn your life around.** Just realizing that abundance is truly there for all of us, and being thankful that you are alive is the key.

CHAPTER 12

Choices

It's Not the Choice That Matters

You wake up in the morning and the world once more beckons you with the never-ending question: "So what's today going to be like and how am I going to get through it? Is it going to be filled with sunshine and roses, rain clouds and bolts of lightning or maybe a combination of the two? Will my journey take me down the yellow brick road or the road less traveled? Am I going to sneak in the back door, go over the top or just slip around the side? So many choices and 'Oh my God,' what if I make the wrong choice or take the wrong turn, will my life be ruined forever?"

Apparently that's what a lot of women must be afraid of or they wouldn't stay stuck in their dead-end jobs, their going-nowhere relationships or their make-do lives. This fear of failure, "making the wrong choice," can be so overwhelming many of us tend to stay stuck by making *no choice* at all! The mere thought of a wrong decision is so paralyzing, we do nothing, and then spend time beating ourselves up for the *no choice* as well!

I remember one particular day when everything in my life seemed to be going wrong. I was sitting with my special friend Nancy, who is a skilled relationship coach gifted with a happy gene, complaining bitterly about the state of my life and all the bad *choices* I had made. After she was sure I was done ranting and raving, she turned to me and said, "Joy darling, there is nothing in the caterpillar that tells you it's going to be a butterfly, nor is there a secret code hidden within any *choice* that will absolutely guarantee you success or failure. *It's Not The Choice, But What You Do With It That Matters.*

So what if you tried something that you thought would make you happier or make things better in your life, and it didn't work out the way you hoped it would? So what if that awesome guy you had future fantasies about turns out to be the biggest jerk, and so what if the last diet you tried left you with a five pound weight gain? So what if you made a few bad choices? You've just got to try again. Try again and again and again.

Why? Because the universe is a big jokester and often times what we think is 'the best thing ever,' turns out to be *at best* a wonderful learning lesson, and 'the worst thing ever' turns out to be a blessing in disguise! To deny yourself the opportunity to have a truly wonderful life just because you are afraid of making a mistake, is like giving up before you've even begun. As a wise woman once said, behind every successful woman is a lot of very unsuccessful experiences."

When you get right down to it and cut away all the fluff, life is all about CHOICE. How you *choose* to act or react affects your moods and how you live your life. Once you decide to "*Choose to*" instead of "*Choose to not*" and to replace "need" with "want," you take back your personal power.

It's Not The Choice, But What You Do With It That Matters, is one of my favorite pearls of wisdom because it really is the credo for a truly &xtraordinary life. When you can take whatever hand fate dealt you and then turn it around to your advantage, when you can take a situation that has the potential of breaking your heart and destroying your spirit and see it as merely another subplot for your "one-woman show," your life will become the greatest show on earth!

"Look for the win in everything," Nancy say's. "Do your grieving, feel your pain, face your disappointments and rejections, and then look for the gifts that always come with your experiences." When you can face anything and everything with this kind of attitude, when you can take a difficult beginning and turn it around to make yourself a winner, there really isn't very much that will ever keep you down for very long.

Make the *choice* to turn your ordinary life into an &xtraordinary one, and watch what you do with that *choice*; it will teach you volumes about what really matters to you. *It's Not The Choice But What You Do With It That Matters*, is like watching the caterpillar turn into the butterfly: an unexplainable magical mystery so symbolic of all that is life. A plain fuzzy thing that can turn into a rainbow of unexpected delight.

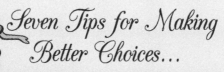

Seven Tips for Making Better Choices...

1. **Trust your intuition.** Inside each of us is an all-knowing wise self. Trust that you know best. Listen to the voice inside that always guides you.

2. **Create your own value system.** When you live out of your integrity and from your values, you never need to be afraid of making a wrong choice.

3. **Make choices that honor who you are.** When you consciously make choices that will better your life and the people in it, there are only good choices.

4. **Take counsel. Include it all.** All the information, opinions and facts you can get. Then armed with the facts, make your decisions and your best choices.

5. **Welcome it all.** There are no bad choices, just one more way to learn. Everything can be seen in a dozen different ways, it's what you do with it that matters.

6. **Choose the life you want,** not the life you've been told you should live or think you should live. When you choose your deepest desire, magic happens.

7. **Choose to learn to love yourself.** Then choose your life from the strength of knowing your worth, and that you always deserve the best for yourself.

CHAPTER 13

Self-Sabotage

Don't Assume Anything

If you were to say to me, what do you think is the worst thing that any woman could possibly do to herself in the form of *SELF-SABOTAGE*, I would have to say it is assuming that others see life exactly the way she does. When you think that others do or should think the way you do, feel the way you do, operate the way you do, have the same standards that you do, etc., etc., it only sets you up for lots of unmet expectations and mucho disappointments. As humbling as it might be to admit, I can't tell you how many times I have felt diminished, rejected, or not validated by someone's action or reaction, or lack of action or reaction to me.

In retrospect, I've learned that most of the abuse I felt was mostly my own creation, and others hadn't done what I had *assumed* they had done. And rarely did they have any idea that I was even feeling the way I did. If I had only had the courage at the time to tell them how I felt, things would have probably been cleared up almost immediately.

61

Years ago I invited a varied group of my friends to come to my house on a rainy Saturday for a trial run on a new seminar that I was giving. My friend Suzanne has been a very highly respected spiritual counselor and holistic healer for many years, and frankly I just *assumed* that she would find this creative stage too boring and would politely decline, but she didn't! At the end of the day, after many hours of sharing my work and getting some really valuable input from all of the participants, I went around and personally thanked each woman individually for being there.

When I finally got around to Suzanne I told her how much I really appreciated her coming, especially since I had really *assumed* that this kind of day was way beyond her. She turned to me and said, "Joy, *Don't Assume Anything*, it's a terrible way to *Sabotage Yourself*. I would never have missed the opportunity to help you bring your important work out to other women, and you should know that about me by now.

When you *assume* anything, you are making an *Ass* out of *U* and *Me*. And if you ever *assume* I feel a particular way about anything, ask me! It's always better to ask someone how they feel or what they mean by what they've said or done, than it is to *assume* anything. If each and every one of us could make it a rule to always have clean and clear communications with everyone in our life, wrong *assumptions* could never be made."

I felt so foolish. In reality she had never done anything for me to have come to those conclusions, so why did I *assume* she wouldn't want to be there? In fact the real question is, why do I always *assume* the worst and consequently end up damaging myself? Beside the bits and pieces of insecurities we all carry around, the only excuse I could give myself is that being a woman I can't stand the unsolved mystery, and I need to have answers for everything.

Unfortunately my first answers always seem to go to the negative before they go to the positive. And if I don't feel like actually communicating with someone or asking for answers I just make up *assumptions* about what's going on, and then I actually believe those *assumptions!* Talk about SELF-SABOTAGE! This must of course, have something to do with some terrible damage that had been done to me once upon a time, that I unfortunately or fortunately can't remember. I mean, what else could it be? Certainly not just my misguided thinking!

Well, thank you Suzanne, because nothing has ever been the same for me ever since. Now whenever I feel my mind and body are telling me that something isn't quite right, I make myself stop and go inside to see if what I am feeling is real. Is it possible that what I am *assuming* may not be based on any reality except the one that I have just made up? Is it possible that I am being just a bit too sensitive or getting plugged in to some old wound that has nothing to do with this particular situation or person?

When I stop making up *assumptions*, I then give all of life and all its participants a chance to give me just what I need from them. When I see myself reverting back to *assuming* things, I stop and remember Suzanne's words and the smile on her face when she said, "*to assume anything makes an Ass out of U and Me; now you wouldn't want that would you?*"

Seven Tips for Not Sabotaging Yourself...

1. **Don't take anything personally.** There is nothing anyone else does because of you, they do it because of themselves and their own insecurities and needs.

2. **Trust your intuition.** Trust that you do know what is the right thing to do. Stop second guessing yourself and trust your own inner wisdom and guidance.

3. **Honor yourself and your uniqueness.** Take care of yourself as you would the most important person. Applaud your accomplishments and acknowledge you.

4. **Don't assume anything.** If you feel like something is wrong and you're feeling uncomfortable, give others a chance to clear it up. Make no assumptions.

5. **Have clear communications.** Ask lots of questions and say what's on your mind. Make sure you understand exactly what's being said or done by others.

6. **Ask for what you want.** Everyone has the right to say yes or no, but you'll never know what they will say if you don't ask! It's just being smart, not pushy.

7. **Be impeccable with your words.** Don't ever use your words against yourself. Use your thoughts and words to empower you, never to disempower.

CHAPTER 14

Acknowledgment
A Personal Love Note

The following story* is a copy of something I wrote a few years ago in my journal and had completely forgotten about it. When I came upon it years later I sent a copy of it to my daughter, and I received the best gift and life lesson in return. Not only did she absolutely love it, (rereading it dozens of times and sharing it with all her friends,) but her reaction taught me how important it is to stop and show others how much we love them while we can; and in ways that will help them remember it for their lifetime. It also showed me how important it is to occasionally stop and acknowledge yourself for a good job well done.

   * "On the day that I turned fifty I awoke with the awe and wonderment of having actually lived a life for fifty years. I closed my eyes and took a rocket ride through the many hills and valleys, stormy oceans and quiet seas, and glimpses of Heaven and hell that life has shown me. When I finally came down to earth, all I could feel was an incredible sense of gratitude and appreciation for the safe and easy journey that God has clearly been guiding me on.

That evening, my wonderful husband gave me a special birthday party at a hotel, filling the room with my loving and adored family and cherished friends. Definitely a great way to enter into a new era!

A couple of days after the celebration some of my friends sent me pictures that they had taken at the party. The first eight times I looked at all the photos I was totally absorbed with who was in the pictures, how they looked and, of course, how I looked. Sorry, I never said I wasn't human. But by the ninth time I started to capture the essence of what these pictures represented to me.

My mother and role-model, still so beautiful at eighty-four, and the reason that I had something to celebrate that night. My brother and dear friend, who has known me for fifty years and somehow still loved me. My gorgeous hunk of a son, who had grown into such an incredible man that I am so proud of. My generous and loving sweetheart of a husband, friends that I had known for ten-twenty-thirty years, and new friendships that had just begun.

But what really stopped me in my tracks and brought me to my knees, was this picture of a beautiful woman named Lindsay, whom I have the pleasure of calling my daughter. Here stood a woman of exceptional qualities who had once just been a seed growing in my belly, a mere thought that had become my dream come true. My contribution to creation, and the innocent receiver of all of the wondrous gifts and lessons that a mother hopes to offer to her daughter for an easier and more joyful life.

When she was born so healthy, pink, and beautiful, I couldn't have been happier or more at peace with the world. I wanted to be everything I felt a good mother could be, and teach her all of the things I felt she needed to know to create a world filled with happiness and joy. As I stared at the picture I realized that looking back at me from the photo was an incredible woman. A woman of strength and compassion, intelligence and humor, a truly beautiful woman inside and out. A woman who was my dream of having a daughter realized, fully grown and smiling back at me with love and confidence. A delicious woman who was about to become the mother of a daughter herself, preparing to give her "dream" many of the same lessons and supportive help that I had hopefully given her.

I started to cry so hard and so loud, I seriously feared that the neighbors could hear me. My body was actually shaking from the force of my tears. But the best part of it all was that I wasn't crying out of sadness or grief, but out of the overwhelming joy of realizing that I had actually done it! I had manifested my dream of seeing my fabulous daughter become a truly special woman!

For the first time that I could remember in a long time, I truly allowed myself to indulge in the delicious joy of wallowing in the sweet scent of accomplishment. I absolutely knew that *no one else* could have taught my daughter her life lessons exactly as I had, not in the way I did.

All of the times that I had wished and hoped, feared and doubted, and been overwhelmed with moments of insecurity of just not knowing if I was ever doing the right thing, came rushing forward. Were my decisions and actions going to help my precious child or damage her for life? As a mother, or father, or anyone who is responsible for raising a child, you never really know for sure "until the cake is baked" how it's all going to turn out.

And then one day you look at a picture of a smiling, self-assured woman who happens to be your daughter, and you know that you "did good." Somehow in all the craziness, you have managed to create an exceptional human being, who is also a wonderful mother, a super daughter, and a terrific friend. *Somehow* it had all turned out just fine.

Whatever my ways were, they were unique to me, and my particular uniqueness had helped to create this absolutely divine human being. Her mannerisms, her smile, her sense of values and compassion, her stubbornness and dislike for cleaning ovens and emptying the dishwasher, were all a part of the lessons I had brought to her. And with it all, she was grand."

The act of mothering another, in any and all of its forms, is the melody to the song of life and can't be ACKNOWL-EDGED enough. But so are all the other hundreds of things women do that makes a difference in the lives of others on this planet. It is so important to stop once in a while and *Acknowledge* yourself for the difference you have made and your contributions in making this world a better place.

I think the time has come for all women to add a new item to our "to do" lists. You know that list that you create every week with all those very important things you need to do with your day? The one that lists exercising time, car pool, luncheon and dinner dates.

To this list you need to add a moment of time when you can go and stand in front of the mirror and say to yourself, "Congratulations! You are one heck of a terrific broad! Whatever you have done in this lifetime you did the best you could with what you had to work with at the time, and you deserve to fully *acknowledge* yourself for that!"

You've done a great job being you, and no one else in the world could have possibly done it any better! And remember, if you can't *acknowledge* yourself then you'll never be able to fully accept the ACKNOWLEDGEMENT of others.

Seven Tips for Better Acknowledgment Skills...

1. **Practice acknowledging yourself for the courage** it takes to just show up for life, when life seems not to be showing up for you. Bravo brave soul!

2. **Practice acknowledging others for their work.** Everyone is on their own journey and deserves to be acknowledged for all their efforts. Go girl!

3. **Everyday acknowledge something you've done.** Don't waste your time and energy looking for someone else to do it, you know and that's enough!

4. **Acknowledgment is a form of acceptance**, and lack of acknowledgment is a form of judgment. Always voice your approval for yourself and for others.

5. **Acknowledgment is a sign of love;** lack of it says I just don't care. Is that the statement you want to say to yourself or to others? Think about it.

6. **Acknowledge everyone you can, when you can.** Find something worth noting about a friend, loved one, business associate, store helper and strangers.

7. **Acknowledge The Source that created us all.** It's important to remember all the gifts and blessings you've been given, and how good you've turned out.

CHAPTER 15

Fuller Life

Take Pleasure Seriously

Do you really want to have a *FULLER LIFE*? I mean a life that is filled with so much more than just daily responsibilities? Then I suggest you start this very minute to *Take Your Pleasure Seriously*, and make sure you enjoy every single moment of it! Fully enjoying yourself with the ordinary and not so ordinary things is serious business, that is if you really want to turn your ordinary life into an *E*xtraordinary one. Yet so many women deny themselves the pleasure of really enjoying the simple pleasure on a daily basis. Why do you think that is?

Well the sad truth is that having a good time makes many of us feel guilty. We feel guilty mainly because we tend to see experiencing pleasure as a moral weakness. Some of us even feel guilty *just thinking about* wanting more pleasure! And if it doesn't actually make us feel guilty, like when we listen to our favorite music or exercising our bodies, then we tend to diminish the pleasure factor and forget to enjoy these everyday experiences that could easily qualify as great moments of joy.

Sometimes we even tell ourselves that we are holding back on pleasure to improve our well-being, but studies have proven that a decline in daily pleasure does more to make us susceptible to catch the common cold, than does an increase in unpleasant events!

For more years than I would like to remember I lived with what I called a scarcity conscious of "not having enough." As sad as it is, many women do. It's the same old story. You think you are either not rich enough or you are not good looking enough, not smart or educated enough, not disciplined or driven enough, or not enough (fill in the blank.) And when you walk around feeling *you're not enough* long enough, then *nothing* is ever enough for you.

And when nothing is ever enough for you, then nothing can ever completely bring you pleasure or joy. You are forever short-changing yourself in the pleasure department and forever your standards of perfection can never quite be met. Because you feel like you're not worthy enough to have more, you feel guilty even wanting more!

And "not worthy enough" was exactly how I was feeling on that cool autumn night when I was explaining to my wise mentor Julia why my winter holiday would have to wait until sometime in the spring when I had accomplished more on my current project. "Joy, my sweet," she began, "Life goes by so very quickly…much too quickly. And no matter how young you might be in your heart, you know it's true, there just isn't enough time to allow yourself that old fantasy conversation of 'when things settle down, when I am in better shape—physically and financially, or when the demands of my life aren't so great, then I'll have lots of time to enjoy more pleasurable things."

As she took another sip of coffee and rearranged herself on the sofa she went on, "But darling, that's just not how it works! There are no guarantees that you will be able to do what you want, how you want, when you are finally ready to do it. Whatever *IT* is. Right now is the only guaranteed time you or anyone else will ever have to do what you want to do." When she said, "You will never be a failure if you are enjoying a *FULLER LIFE* by *Taking Pleasure Seriously*," her words of wisdom became my new and forever mantra.

I now *Take Pleasure* so *Seriously* it is factored into my work week, just like I do with my social, business, and health care appointments. I now give myself permission to accept and acknowledge my worthiness in enjoying as much pleasure as I possibly can from every single moment of my life.

So how do you begin to have a *Fuller Life* and *Take Pleasure Seriously*? By starting to listen to your body. It's amazing the clues your body will give to you if you only begin to pay attention to it. And if you afraid of having too much pleasure, don't be, because you can't. If you did, it would no longer be pleasurable!

You need to find your bliss point, like one fiddles with a new recipe. Adding a little of this and a little less of that, working with your enjoyment buds to find the most pleasurable balance. Once you have found out what brings you joy, don't take away from your pleasure by measuring it's value or worth. The time you are enjoying wasting, is not wasted time at all, it has purpose.

Pleasure is as vital for a *Fuller life* and your well-being, as is sleep for your mind and body at the end of an active day. One is necessary to complete the other. And to paraphrase what it says in the Talmud, one of the most cherished books of wisdom in the Jewish religion, "When your days are done and you are standing in front of the Lord, you won't be asked how long and hard you've worked, or how much money you have made, or even how many people you have helped along the way. Instead you will be asked how much joy and pleasure have you had in your lifetime, and if not enough, why didn't you enjoy yourself more?"

So whether you spend the day just puttering around the house, searching for treasures through the flea markets, painting landscape or just lying in the sun sipping lemonade, it really doesn't matter, as long as its gives you pleasure and positively affects the quality of your day!

Henry David Thoreau summed it up best when he said, "It is something to be able to paint a particular picture or carve a statue, and to make a few objects beautiful, but it is far more glorious to carve and paint the very atmosphere and medium through which we look…to affect the quality of the day. That is the highest of art." Begin to have a *FULLER LIFE* by *Taking Pleasure Seriously*, and who knows, maybe you'll become the next Michelangelo!

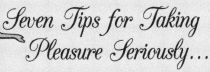

Seven Tips for Taking Pleasure Seriously...

1. **Pleasure helps us find our genius.** It's usually in the middle of having the best of times that we open ourselves up to our unlimited potential and dreams.

2. **Pleasure is the balancer between work and life.** Without something to take us away from the stress and demands of life, "Jackie becomes a very dull girl."

3. **Pleasure gives us time to idle.** Daydreaming helps us develop new ideas as our problems incubate and creativity flows. So pleasure your way to success!

4. **Pleasurable times help us relax, replenish, and revitalize our human spirit.** It helps us clean out the mental cobwebs and think more clearly.

5. **Pleasure helps to keep enthusiasm up and alive.** When you love what you do, all else will follow. It's the secret elixir to a life filled with joy.

6. **Pleasure is fun and we all need fun in our lives.** Life can be tough and we all need to find ways to rise above life's ups and downs. Take it seriously!

7. **Taking pleasure seriously is an important step** in turning an ordinary life into an Extraordinary one. It's the spark that lights the fire within your heart.

CHAPTER 16

Stop Worrying

Relax and Trust

Every now and then you are lucky enough to meet a special person that just by knowing them, you grow and become more of who you want to be. One of my lucky days was when I met my friend Gerri. A great lady for a lot of different reasons, but the one quality that has always impressed me the most is her ability to keep her sense of humor and positive attitude no matter how many curve balls the universe seems to throw her way. I first met Gerri when I was living in The Big Apple and we were both members of a women's group that met once a month for fourteen years. After meeting for fourteen years, you sure do get to know someone.

One night after one of our monthly meetings, as Gerri and I were walking down the street on our way home, I started complaining about some problem I was having. Without saying a word, Gerri spontaneously gave me a comforting hug and with a wink of her eye, placed a small printed card in my hand with the words *Relax and Trust* on it. With that she blew me a kiss goodbye as she ran to catch the rare cab on a busy night in NYC. Her quick getaway left me with my own thoughts and the time to ponder exactly what this message meant.

By the time the next day had arrived I had some of my own answers, but my curiosity was piqued over why Gerri was carrying cards with such a message on them. So I gave her a call. She was delighted that she had sparked my interest and went on to share an experience that had transformed her life.

She said that it all began at a time in her life when she was really feeling down and everything that she wanted seemed destined never to come true. She had been a single mother raising her son alone for a long time and doing all of the things that are necessary to do that well, but she was getting just plain tired of it all. She was tired of dating guys that weren't marriage material, tired of working so hard to support herself and her son, and just plain tired of the general rat race.

"As hokey as it might seem, I just wanted some direction and some answers, so I went to a psychic! Well, I didn't talk to her for very long before she made me a believer. She proceeded to rattle off all kinds of facts about things that I had never even hinted at. So of course I had to ask her my all important burning question, 'When was I ever going to meet Mr. Right?'

For a very long time she said nothing, which made me very nervous, but as it turned out she was concentrating on seeing my future. With a very deep far away voice she said that my soul mate was coming. She told me that he was getting himself ready for me and that he was tidying up his life, and I was to be patient. Then with an all-knowing look she smiled and said, 'Gerri *STOP WORRYING*, just *Relax and Trust*, it's all going to happen for you.'

As I left her place and went out into the sunshine, suddenly everything became crystal clear. I didn't have to worry about anything and I didn't have to do anything either, *except* to simply *Relax and Trust*. Everything was being taken care of for me by a power too great for any of us to ever fully understand. All the energy and control I had always thought I needed to exert in order to make things happen the way I wanted them to, had only been blocking the natural flow of what was meant to be. I had actually been getting in my own way, keeping away what I wanted most of all!"

Shortly after the meeting with the psychic Gerri met the love of her life and they have just recently celebrated their fifteenth wedding anniversary. The message the psychic gave her, to just *Relax and Trust,* gave her the courage to STOP WORRYING and let her intentions magnetize to her, her greatest desire. She now believes that once you can allow yourself to surrender your need to manipulate and control the outcome of your life to a higher power, life becomes so much easier.

When you can *Relax and Trust* into knowing that *everything* is happening exactly as it is meant to, and that you are doing the best you can with what you have at this moment in time, *E*xtraordinary things can happen! Now if that's not a reason to *Relax and Trust*, I don't know what is!

Seven Tips for Helping You Relax and Trust...

1. **Seek out solitude.** Go sit in the garden, take a walk, or indulge yourself with a hot soak in the tub. Find alone time to relax and trust into your dreams .

2. **Ask yourself what it is you really want,** not what someone else wants for you. Then relax and trust that the universe will deliver your true intentions.

3. **Tune into yourself.** Exercise your trust muscle by listening to your all-knowing inner voice. All the right answers are waiting within. Relax and Trust.

4. **Forgive yourself** for all the times when you were too afraid or insecure to relax and trust yourself or the universe. Trust and act on your own beliefs.

5. **Learn to enjoy the process.** Everything has a reason for being. Relax and trust that it will all work out fine and eventually it all will.

6. **Live more authentically.** Even if it stir up anxiety and discomfort, it will also give you great joy and power. Trust the process—just relax and trust.

7. **Recognize your own truth, act on that knowledge.** Have the courage to take responsibility for your choices, and then relax and trust into your wisdom.

CHAPTER 17

Fear

What About This Concerns You?

FEAR is such an insidious thing. It comes over you like a black cloud, and no matter how much you try, you can't see the light at the end of the tunnel through all the heavy darkness. And no matter how many well placed or brilliant words your friends or family try to give you to help you get past it, in reality the only way out is through it. Yet even as I am writing these words I know that "there is nothing to *Fear* but *Fear* itself," is often easier said than done.

For more years than I care to remember, I seem to have repeatedly had two "*Fear* day/nightmares." One of them is that I will forget something unbelievably important, like the time or day I need to take a final exam to pass a particular course in order to graduate, or the location of some important event I am supposed to attend. I see myself running around like a crazy person looking for the right building or room where this event is happening. I am petrified that the rug will be pulled out from under me because I missed it, and all my life will fall apart and shatter like a precious Waterford crystal vase dropped on a tiled floor.

The second one happens when I am very much awake, AKA day/nightmare. It usually occurs on a day that's like a Sunday afternoon, when I am free to design exactly how I want to spend each moment of my day. A day planned with no work, and no real responsibilities to be anywhere or do anything for anyone else. One of those rare days that women never seem to get enough of. A day to pamper and rejuvenate yourself for whatever else is coming next.

All of a sudden I am taken over by the fear that someone is going to come knocking on my door, literally speaking, and stop me from enjoying this precious rare time. Even though I know that neither of these fear dreams are based on reality, they sure do feel real in my body when I am going through them.

My turning point came one day when I was reading an article about a beloved spiritual teacher, and the words of wisdom she had shared with her students about how to handle *FEAR*. Her approach was one I had never heard before, and yet it greatly helped me to deal with my *Fear* from then on. She said, "Never ask yourself what it is you *Fear*, instead ask yourself *What Is It That Concerns You?*"

She went on to say that "all thoughts put out into the universe will eventually return to you, because energy always makes a loop back until it returns to the source. Fearful thoughts based on negative beliefs can be damaging and constrictive, certainly not the energy that you want to repeatedly surround you. The energy that is sourced from a concern to see what's under those beliefs and why they frighten you, is energy in search of a hidden treasure in the form of an answer, and therefore is positive and reinforcing. Notice the *Fear*, how it is making you feel and what it is doing to your body. Then ask yourself the question, *What*

Is It That Concerns Me? What am I really afraid will happen?"

Hmm, now that's an intriguing question. What is really going on here that is concerning me? Well the most obvious thing that I could think of, is that I am concerned that I will get carried away with having too much fun. That I will somehow forget something so very important, that it will alter my life negatively forever. Someone will interrupt it or take away my special day, and worst of all, I am going to let them! As I went deeper into my thoughts, I realized that *I am concerned* with my ability to create and maintain boundaries that will protect my interests. In other words, to be able to say No, still be liked, and not feel guilty for saying No!

The more I repeated the question *What Is It That Concerns You?*, the closer I got to the truth. I was suffering from a life-long disease many ordinary women on the road to an $\mathcal{E}$xtraordinary life suffer from, which is "the need to please other people." I have been so concerned my whole life with making sure I pleased other people and doing what is requested of me, that even when there are no real demands, I still suffer from a knee-jerk reaction to make everybody happy.

I am filled with the *Fear* that I won't be doing what "I should," and if I don't do the right thing, *or whatever* it is everyone wants and expects me to do, then obviously the entire world will shout out in agreement, "*She's a fraud, selfish, and not that wonderful, thoughtful human being you think she is!*"

This observation was a turning point in my life. Not only did probing my mind with the question of *What Is It That Concerns You?* help to take the charge off of my *Fears*, it also freed me from the bonds of not knowing what's really behind those and other *Fears*. When you take the time to stop, listen, and pay close attention to what your inner voice is telling you, you can often find many answers you've been looking for.

This simple straightforward question has the power to transform your fearful thoughts into thoughts that focus on discovering the source of your *Fears*. Filling your mind with the question and the search for the answers, is a refreshing change from wallowing in those dense limiting feelings of *FEAR*.

And sometimes what you discover is so enlightening, it has the potential of changing your life forever. It's just another example of how an ordinary woman can have an *E*xtraordinary life…if that's what concerns you.

Seven Tips for Handling Your Fears...

1. **Hope and faith can transform fear.** Use your belief in a higher power to help you move forward. Life can be scary and tough without faith and hope.

2. **Everyone has a certain level of fear.** Dealing with it includes first noticing what pushes your buttons, how you control it, and how you manage it.

3. **Facing fear is a work in progress.** Until you try you'll never know what you can endure or how capable you are in handling problems. Stay strong.

4. **F.E.A.R—false expectations appearing real.** It may be an oldie but goodie, but it's true. You have nothing to fear but fear itself. Think positively.

5. **Fear is often associated with taking a risk,** yet it's often that risk-taking action that frees and moves you away from what you fear the most. Just do it.

6. **Fear often paralyzes you, don't let it.** Do anything that you can to change your environment and your state of mind. Change combats fear.

7. **Remember all the things you have ever feared** that never happened the way you thought they would? Fear is bigger in your mind then in reality.

CHAPTER 18

Staying Open

You Just Don't Know

How do you think we all caught this killer disease? Through bugs brought over in plants, bees that were flying south, or maybe the north winds that blew it over the entire country? What am I talking about? I am talking about that killer disease that makes all of us so sure that *we know exactly* how things are going to happen or be. And when things turn out differently than we expected, we become totally devastated, disappointed, and disillusioned. The disease I am referring to is called "*I Know.*" "*I Know* this is going to happen this way, and *I Know* it's not going to happen that way. *I Know* this means this, and *I know* that means that." When asked "How do you know?" You say, "*I just Know!*"

A couple of years ago I was having tea with my girl-friend Cathy, who had just come out of a succession of some pretty difficult years. Because of various circumstances, she and her husband had gone from having a fairly affluent lifestyle to barely getting by. After many years of going through these rough times, things finally turned around.

"So now that you're on the other side of all the problems," I asked her as she passed the cookies, "what do you think you've learned from all this?"

"The biggest lesson I've learned" she said, "was to never think you know anything, because *You Just Don't Know!* And the biggest problem with thinking you know what is going to happen, is that you shut yourself down to any other new possibilities. By not living in the question or the present moment you are already living and creating your future conclusions.

Besides I am convinced that when the "*I Know*" has any negative conclusions, you only help to manifest your worst fears into reality. It is so important to just *STAY OPEN*." Which reminded me of a great story.

"One day a Chinese man called Aoki-san was sitting on his porch when he saw his neighbors horse break loose from the stable and run away. He came banging on his neighbor's door shouting, "Dear neighbor, come look. Something bad has happened. Your horse has just run away."

The neighbor looked at the gate, and then looked at him, and simply replied, "I don't know if it's bad and I don't know if it's good."

The next day the horse returned with the most beautiful wild white stallion running beside him. When Aoki-san saw this he shouted, "Oh, neighbor come look at your good fortune! Your horse has returned with another beautiful horse! This is so good."

'Yes my friend it's true. The horse is certainly beautiful, but I don't know if it's good and I don't know if it's bad," said the neighbor as he tied the horses up.

The next day, the neighbor's son decided to ride the wild stallion, which didn't like that a bit and threw him off. As the boy lay on the ground screaming from a broken leg, Aoki yelled, "Oh neighbor what a terrible horse. He broke your son's leg, it's so bad."

"Yes," sighed the neighbor. "It's true my son has a broken leg, but I don't know if it's good, and I don't know if it's bad."

The very next day, the captain of the local army came to recruit all of the eligible men of the land for his troop, which was equivalent to a death sentence because of the guerrilla war that was going on. But since the boy had a broken leg and was considered damaged goods, the captain decided not to take him.

"Oh neighbor how good this is. How terrible it would have been if your son had to go in the army. They all get killed," shouted Aoki-san.

As the neighbor turned to go inside he looked up and smiled at old Aoki-san, and said, "Yes, it's true my friend. My son didn't go to the army and for that I am grateful, but as all things in life, one never knows till our days are done whether anything that happens to us is really good or really bad."

So what is the learning lesson Cathy and Aoki-san have in common? It's that even though it is human nature to want to help create or design your future, you need to remember that it rarely happens or turns out exactly as you had assumed it would. When you can begin to believe in the idea of *STAYING OPEN* and that you *Just Don't Know*, you free yourself up to living your life in the moment and all the magical moments yet to come.

Once you realize that all of the circumstances and the ultimate outcome of your life are pretty much out of your control, and that all you can ever do is the best you can do with what you have to work with in the present moment, life becomes much simpler. The perceived past and the possible future, which is usually the foundation for your knowing, no longer has value in your decision making process.

STAYING OPEN to the idea that *You Just Don't Know,* lets you stay open to all the unexpected magical things that can possibly turn an ordinary woman's life into an *&*xtraordinary one. Surrendering yourself to a higher force that has a wisdom that we will never know or fully understand, can be the most freeing and empowering thing you will ever do for yourself. Why not give it try…I mean really, *"You just don't know!"*

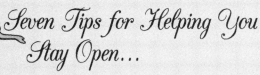

Seven Tips for Helping You Stay Open...

1. **Pay attention and watch.** Since we don't ever know for sure what's really going to happen, stay open and enjoy watching life unfold at your feet.

2. **Life is a jokester, enjoy the joke.** Oftentimes what we think will be wonderful is not and our disappointments become our greatest gift.

3. **Practice good listening techniques.** Listen for more than what is said. Because beyond the words is often the truth of the real message.

4. **Keep your mind open.** Because when your mind is closed you think you know the answer and you are often closing the door to other possibilities.

5. **Magic and miracles are the eternal mysteries of life.** Knowing that you just don't know or even understand is an important step in staying open.

6. **Let go.** The only thing that you know for sure, is that the outcome will look different than your vision—stay open to the essence of what you want.

7. **Don't take life or yourself too seriously.** Everything is temporary and nothing lasts forever. Staying open to everything is the answer.

CHAPTER 19

Being Centered

Journal Your Troubles Away

It doesn't matter how many books you've read or tapes you've listened to, workshops or yoga classes you've attended, or hours you've spent in meditation with hot bubble baths…*things will happen.* It could be feeling disillusioned over another unmet expectation or circumstances out of your control, or experiencing some form of rejection or finally admitting to the truth; that sometimes, you can't even depend on yourself to honor your own agreements. *Whatever*, the buttons get pushed and you are totally plugged in. From that moment on, your mind becomes obsessed with finding the answers that will help make you feel better and finally being able to put the growling ugly dark beast to rest.

For most of us the process is pretty much the same. First we allow ourselves to feel the hurt and pain for an open-ended amount of time. Then we get on the phone with our top shelf main support team for a shot of the triple S— Solace, Sympathy, and Support. And if their words and ears are not enough, we have all been known to move onto the third, fourth and even the "mere acquaintance" shelf, just to vent and be heard. And of course that doesn't count all the hours we spend talking to ourselves until we are sick and tired of hearing our own voice!

Now even though these methods certainly have their place in helping with the clearing process and should never be completely eliminated, I think I have come upon an easier and possibly even more effective way to finally get these feelings out of your mind and body. My solution is to sit down and *Journal Your Troubles Away.*

Simply take a pen or pencil to a book with blank sheets of paper you will call your journal, and proceed to write out every single thought, feeling, and emotion that you have on whatever is going in your life that is bothering you. Write for as long as you want or need to, just don't stop until you feel some sort of mental and physical relief.

The concept of writing down your feelings into a private journal is to create a safe outlet to cleanse and free yourself from those obsessive thoughts and feelings that can hurt you or someone else, emotionally or physically. The idea is to clear the way for you to return to the state of *BEING CENTERED.*

Now there are different schools of thought on the *"what, where, and how"* of doing this. Since I personally have no desire to return to the scene of the crime, so to speak, my preference is not to write with my treasured special pen or put my most icky emotions into a beautifully bound journal. I prefer a plain soft covered pad that I can just throw away when it's filled up, just as I plan to do with the problems!

OK, so here's the drill. Make yourself comfortable in your bed, a chair, or a sofa with good lighting next to it. A nice quiet place where you can be assured of no interruptions. A hot cup of herbal tea would be nice here or a cup of your favorite coffee, but not necessary. Once you are settled in and have gathered your thoughts, begin to write down whatever comes into your mind, using the simplest and most straight forward language.

Try to express every thought and feeling you have on the subject, and please no editing, since the intention is for no one else to read this but you! It's important to write down how you truly feel about everything, without any concern for the quality of your penmanship or spelling. The sole purpose of this exercise is to get those restrictive feelings out of your body, and then hopefully with a clearer head, help you find some answers or solutions that will get you back to *BEING CENTERED*.

This is the place where it's necessary for you to become your own tough love therapist, the one who asks the really uncomfortable difficult questions. Then you have to become the willing patient who "speaks" the truth about what's really going on, and how you are truly feeling about it all. Once you begin to *Journal Your Troubles Away* don't be afraid to ask the really hard, even painful questions. like "why did this happen? What do I really want? What is getting in my way of having what I really want? Or the one that always separates the girls from the women, "What is my responsibility in all of this?"

I know how much it hurts to relive the painful moments and disappointments of your life, but it's better to go into the pain and really feel it for the moment, than it is to carry it around for days, months, or even years without closure. Nothing else in the world has as much power to keep your spirits down, weigh heavier on your heart, or give you more back and stomach aches, than carrying around all the unmonitored damage that human beings can so easily give to one another.

Journaling Your troubles Away can truly be a purification process and one not to be taken lightly. It can be the very action that can lighten your heart and return you to *BEING CENTERED*, as well as making you capable of handling whatever else the day may bring. Do it when you first wake up in the morning or do it right before you go to bed at night. Do it when you are home alone, riding on the train, in a cab, or on a plane. Do it anytime and anywhere you can, especially when your body tells you that *something's wrong* and it's time to deal with it. Listen carefully because your body will always tell you what's really going on.

Nothing is more powerful in turning an ordinary woman's life into an *Extraordinary* one, than having and using the tools that can help her in *BEING CENTERED*. When you are operating from a calm centered place, everything else flows more naturally.

Journaling Your Troubles Away is one of the best solutions I've found for clearing away the negativity and regaining your personal power. Besides, the world can always use another writer. So why not begin today to become the next Pulitzer Prize winning author? I suggest you start with *Journal Your Troubles Away!*

Seven Tips for Journaling Problems Away...

1. **Journaling first thing in the morning** is a great way to get rid of yesterday's problems and begin the day anew. Begin by just letting the words flow.

2. **Journal just for your eyes only—no one else's.** When you write with the freedom of knowing that no one else will read it—you can tell your truth.

3. **Journal in a safe and comfortable place.** When we feel comfortable and safe we feel free to let our true selves be true to ourselves.

4. **Journal for at least three minutes or more.** Give yourself a fair amount of time to examine your issues and then to express them fully.

5. **Use a pen and pad that you can throw away.** That way you feel no qualms in throwing away your troubles and concerns with it.

6. **Play doctor. Ask the hard questions** and be willing to say what's really on your mind. It's a sure way to get to know the real you.

7. **Journal whenever and wherever** the mood strikes you. If you feel the need, then the need is there. Journal and enjoy the results.

CHAPTER 20

Disappointment

Let It Be

After all these years, it never fails to surprise me how plugged in I can get when someone does something to personally hurt or upset me. I am referring to those times when the least attractive part of your personality decides to rear it's ugly head, because of a particular person or situation that has really hurt or *disappointed* you.

Various emotions are rising to the surface, emotions that you had hoped and prayed that you had certainly learned how to deal with by now. Feelings like anger, jealousy, rage and revenge, the need to control, manipulate or the idea of doing some form of damage to this particular person or situation, are running rampant inside your head. Base emotions that you find disgusting when you see them in others, now seem even more despicable as they come seeping out from some dark murky place buried deep inside of you.

"Where did that reaction come from? I thought for sure I was *way above* that sort of thing. Is this one of those divine moments when I am forced to see just how 'un-evolved' I really am?" Suddenly your personal growth seems nonexistent and you've become someone you barely recognize! Thank God for that! But what do you do with those feelings of DISAPPOINTMENT when they feel so big and overpowering? How does one keep herself centered and forgiving when she feels so betrayed and let down? *Let it Be!*

One day last June, I had a so-called friend do something so hurtful to me that all I could feel for hours was this overwhelming feeling of betrayal and *Disappointment* for the way I had been treated. And worst of all I was even more *disappointed* in myself for the revenge I wanted to seek, and how vulnerable I still was to such behavior.

My immediate response was certainly not what I would have hoped for from "a woman who thought herself to be on the path of spiritual evolvement" for so many years of her life. No matter how well I thought I could handle such a situation in theory, in the moment of upset, all my spiritual wisdom seemed to have left me. So out of total frustration with my exposed "dark shadow side," I decided to take a walk on the beach to clear my head.

After reviewing all of the different options that I could think of to either change, understand, or rise above these feelings, I had to admit that nothing I was doing seemed to be working or making me feel any better. Still I knew that if I didn't finally find some permanent solution for handling all of my DISAPPOINTMENTS, not just this one, these lousy feelings would return again and again, but what? As I began milling over this idea I suddenly began to hear a voice singing softly at first, than louder and louder inside my head. *"Let It Be, Let It Be, Let It Be, Let It Be, speaking words of wisdom, Let It Be!"*

"Oh my God," I thought to myself, "I have somehow channeled John Lennon himself to deliver this important message to me!" (Don't you just love a vivid imagination?) And then the voice started to speak to me.

"Give yourself a break kid; you are only human. Sometimes the best you can do is to acknowledge that when someone has hurt you it hurts. Sometimes the only lesson to be learned from such experiences is who you don't want to have in your life and why, and then thank the universe for giving you that gift and the opportunity to do something about it! Right now, the best thing you can do is to forgive yourself for being such a sensitive and open-hearted woman, and then just *Let It Be!*"

Wow, this was really cool. I've heard of other people channeling relatives or unknown spirits, but it's not very often that you get John Lennon to help you find your way! So with that chosen belief in my head (each to their own) John went on to say, "So what if your so-called friend has turned out to be a rat-fink, and what she did to you has left you feeling hurt and *disappointed* and all you want is sweet revenge. Instead of burying your heels into your "rightness" and trying to create the support you need to justify your feelings of *Disappointment*, or looking for ways to carry out some sweet revenge and ultimately being a way you really don't want to be, how about trying to just *Let It Be.*"

People will do things to you and situations will come into your life oftentimes just to help you grow. It may not always seem that way, and sometimes it can take quite awhile before you can really understand that. But once you can see that in all situations each of us is only being ourselves and responding according to our own programming, the sooner you will realize that most of your *DISAPPOINT-MENTS* are caused by your expectations of others according to your rules.

That doesn't mean that you have to accept being treated badly. It just means that once you can see and understand each person's limitations, the sooner you can make the choice of whether or not you want them in your life. And the sooner you get that message, the sooner you can get back into the groove of turning your ordinary life into an &xtraordinary one. As my new best friend John Lennon once said, "the best way to do that is to just *Let It Be. Let It Be, Let It Be, Let It Be, Let It Be…* remember these pearls of wisdom next time, and *LET IT BE!*"

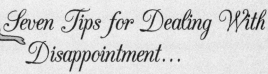

Seven Tips for Dealing With Disappointment...

1. **Make a conscious choice to shed outdated beliefs** that keep you stuck in limited thinking. Open your mind and heart to new ideas and then let it be.

2. **Look at your problem retrospectively,** will this issue really bother you in ten-fifteen years? If the honest answer is no...let it be.

3. **Try deep breathing to center your thoughts.** When you feel caught up in the craziness, count to 10 as you slowly exhale —deep in—slowly out. Let it be.

4. **Practice the art of detachment.** Remember a time in your life when you got what you wanted without being attached to the end result. Let it be.

5. **Find a way to move on** even if things don't work out the way you want. It's a great way to open the door to letting more of what you want come in. Let it be.

6. **Try trusting being yourself.** Once you do, things just seem to fall into place more easily. Almost miraculously you find your answers. Let it be.

7. **Hear the words of wisdom...let it be.** There is no payoff on holding on to upsets or letting it run you for days. It really is wisdom to just let it be.

CHAPTER 21

Great Friendships

Whistle Clean

Wow, have things changed, thank God! Just to think that it wasn't so long ago that so many women thought all women were either their direct competition or arch enemies, and men were their best friends. Clearly somewhere along the way women en masse agreed to believe a really great snow job. For years it kept women at an arms distance from the love, support, and sisterhood of understanding that only women can give to each other, and life was a lot more difficult and lonely. Just imagine how much women would have missed if that myth hadn't been dispelled! But even though women are clearly the best thing since sliced whole wheat bread, we still have a lot to learn, and too often we fall into nasty old habits.

One of those nasty old habits that I am referring to is trying to keep everything in our lives nice and neat at all costs. We will do whatever we can to avoid those uncomfortable confrontations, and then make excuses for things others did to us or didn't do for us, just so we don't have to deal with it! It seems so much easier to just let things slide, even when it ends up causing us ulcers, upset stomachs, and costly phone calls to our support team. But as we all know, trying to break any lifetime habit ain't easy. It takes a real commitment to a higher commitment, like being your authentic self.

The women's group that I was a member of for fourteen years until I moved, which by the way, was fondly called The Bliss Group, gave me many gifts. I highly recommend other women forming or joining a group of women who come together to learn and support each other's personal growth. Because of the different kinds of energy and knowledge that women brought to the group, the conversations were always quite spirited, and often times confrontational.

One night after having one of those spirited discussions about how couples communicate, I decided to have a couples party at my home to continue the discussion. My vision was an evening where we could learn valuable information and explore more deeply the subject of making relationships work by adding the male energy.

At the next meeting I noticed that my Bliss sister Niki was being very distant and cool to me, and for the life of me I really couldn't understand why. During our opening "sharing session," where everybody shares what's been going on in their lives over the last month, Niki said that she wanted to tell us about another group that she was involved in.

She went on to tell us that she and some other friends had started a group where their main objective was to learn how to communicate better with each other by always speaking their truth. Their mutual agreement was that no matter how uncomfortable, awkward, or embarrassing it might feel to either party to always speak your truth, it was the only way to create worthwhile relationships. And that included all those little white lies that we don't always seem to count. The belief being that when you don't tell the truth, it depletes your energy and damages your relationships with others. So they created a phrase to live by called *Whistle Clean*.

Whistle Clean is an unspoken agreement between two people who are committed to having honest and authentic open communications, as well as GREAT FRIENDSHIPS. Being *Whistle Clean* means having the courage to tell a friend when they say or do something that hurts or bothers you, how you really feel about it. Caring enough to tell another how you feel about what they have done to you, and giving them a chance to explain, apologize or change it, instead of building a case against them, is what *Great Friendships* and great relationships are all about.

Then Niki turned to me and said, " Joy I have to be *Whistle Clean* with you and tell you just how hurt I was that you didn't include me in your "couples communication party." I understand that I may not be in relationship at the moment, and I know that was the reason why I wasn't invited. But I certainly have been before, and I could have brought a male friend and given some interesting insights. I felt that it was insensitive and very excluding."

Not only did I understand, but I felt really terrible for my oversight and apologized immediately. But the bigger picture had been shown to all of us. Being *Whistle Clean* is really the only way to create great relationships, and it goes both ways. Niki went on to say that if she had been playing full out, she would have called me before the party and told me how she felt, knowing that I would have cleared up things right then and there. But like everyone else at one time or another, being right for being wronged, feels so good and seems so much more important then taking the opportunity to clear things up does.

When you are committed to being *Whistle Clean* with the people in your life it makes you think twice about what you say and do, as well as giving you the freedom to be exactly who you want to be. When you know your friends will surely bring you back to center if you slip, and that you have the open invitation to do the same with them, it makes it much easier to speak your truth as well as to deal with those uncomfortable confrontations.

As you are learning, for a woman to turn her ordinary life into an &xtraordinary one includes many different facets. Developing GREAT FRIENDSHIPS and great relationships that are *Whistle Clean,* is an important part to practicing the *art of living well!*

Why not follow Lauren Bacal's lead and try doing what she said to Bogey in one of their best movies, "Just put your lips together and blow." Try whistling the new catchy tune called Having an &xtraordinary Life and enjoy having *Great Friendships!*

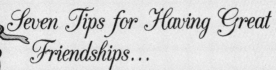

Seven Tips for Having Great Friendships...

1. **True friendships are built on solid foundations.** A true friend will always want to understand how you really feel about everything...no matter what.

2. **Respect for each other is essential in friendships.** Expressing your differences or even disagreements with respect, is a good thing for great friendships.

3. **Sharing your most personal information** with a good friend and knowing that it will be held in the strictest confidence creates great friendships.

4. **Supporting a friend in their time of need,** and being by their side to give them whatever they need—no matter what the circumstances are—that's a friend.

5. **See your friends in their highest light.** When you choose to see the best in your friends, you hold up the mirror for them to reflect their best back to you.

6. **Always listen for the unspoken request.** The words that say, I need or want you in my life now for whatever reason...please say yes and please be there.

7. **Let your friends be there for you.** Everyone wants to be needed so let them. Don't abuse the privilege or be an energy sapper...we all need boundaries.

CHAPTER 22

Self-Care

Be Frivolous and Decadent

It's vital. It is absolutely necessary, with the same importance that you put on eating healthy foods, taking your vitamins, and adding daily exercise to your life, for you to set aside a few hours (or more) one day a week to do something to take care of yourself that is considered totally *Frivolous and Decadent*. Now for some women this idea seems absolutely absurd. Since somewhere along the line they have connected the idea of *SELF-CARE* with how much they can accomplish in a day.

The prevailing thought being that if you can hold down a job, take care of a home and family, be involved in outside activities, *plus* do all the necessary things that you need to do just to keep yourself alive and functioning in some state of health without falling apart; Then you must be doing a great job. To think of doing something just to please yourself seems so *"frivolous and decadent,"* it's almost impossible to imagine. With this lifestyle being a role model for success, it's no wonder that so many people think having an

Extraordinary life is a fantasy. Especially when their main concern is simply keeping all the balls in the air!

If this resembles your life in anyway, and if at this moment you really don't see how you can change things (at least not right now) then maybe this is the time to consider the idea of doing something that is totally radical. Something like factoring *you* into your daily schedule. Make a note at the top of the to-do list today that says, "*Self-Care*, must do something special for me today." Then find that time to do something that is totally *Frivolous and Decadent* just to please yourself!

Why does it have to be *Frivolous and Decadent?* Because most of us are so "others oriented," you might pretend that errands and necessary things are the same, but trust me they're not. Doing something that is *just for you* that may seem a bit foolish, silly or wasteful, is a much bigger statement. It says to you and the world, "I am as important as everyone and everything else in my life. As much as I am giving to the rest of the world, I sure as heck deserve to give to me!"

So how do you begin? How about doing something girlie, like spending sometime during the day in front of the mirror playing with different hair styles and new make-up? Or maybe taking a solitary drive or walk around town without any concern for the time or where you are actually going. Another suggestion is to find a cozy chair in a quiet corner, with a nice hot cup of coffee or an iced tea, and get on the phone.

Start connecting with all those friends or family members that you haven't had anytime to have a really good conversation with in ages. Write in your journal, start to write your book or write a letter to someone who would be so surprised and delighted to receive it. Maybe take up a hobby, something you have wanted to try to make or do forever, but didn't ever seem to have the time. Whatever it is, do something just for you!

When you take seriously the suggestion of your own *Self-Care* by doing something that is thought of as *Frivolous and Decadent*, you are confirming with the universe that you do indeed deserve more joy in your life. That your personal worth isn't attached to how much bacon you bring home, how much you've accomplished in the world, or how many people you take care of or responsibilities you have taken on. Just being you is enough to deserve a reward!

And the next time that you notice your consumption of pleasure is way below the necessary requirement, take out your appointment book and pencil in time for *you*. Make a point of doing something that is all about you taking care of you—not anyone else. Something that is totally *Frivolous and Decadent*, that couldn't possible look or feel like work. If that Jewish/Catholic/Protestant "guilt thing" starts to kick in, and you still feel as if you need an excuse to tell *whomever* why you are spending so much time doing such silly *"frivolous and decadent"* things for yourself, simple smile and say, "I have to. Dr. Joy said that it's vital for my health!"

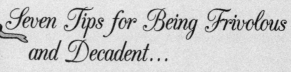

Seven Tips for Being Frivolous and Decadent...

1. **Don't do anything that feels like responsibility.** The mental benefits of doing things frivolous and decadent, is that it takes you away from drudgery.

2. **Do things that feel childlike.** Kids love doing things that are frivolous and decadent. It makes you feel free, limitless and fill of giggles and joy.

3. **Enjoy little pleasures,** like walking in dewy grass barefoot, eating an ice cream sundae on Monday. Little pleasures can be delicious and naughty!

4. **Enjoy big pleasures,** like going off to a health spa, or parachute jumping, or doing a cooking course in Paris. Just because you can and you deserve it!

5. **Create an at-home-spa.** Pull out the scented everything—candles, oils, incense, perfume, and use them. Then go somewhere else in your mind.

6. **Use your imagination** when you absolutely can't get away. Pretend that you are doing your chores like an actor in a movie—just for the fun of it!

7. **Make your own list** of things that are frivolous and decadent. And one by one, check them off as you do them. Taking care of yourself changes your life!

CHAPTER 23

Positive Change

Change the Energy

As they say, some days are barely worth getting up for,
and the anger and rage that permeates the air we breath is
almost suffocating. *Everyone* seems to have a legitimate
excuse for their own bad behavior. The man at the news-
stand is curt because he had a fight with his wife, and the
waitress at lunch had no patience with the amount of time
it's taking you to make a decision. Her feet hurt, and she
wants to be home playing with her kids. And let us not
forget the guy in the blue Buick who is acting out with car
rage because he's late for whatever, and you're in his way.
Whatever the reason, anyone of us could certainly get a
heck of a lot of validation from whomever, for responding
in return with the same anger or rage.

But that certainly is not going to make your day, no less
your life *Extraordinary*, now is it? To do that you would
need to be willing to take responsibility for activating some
POSITIVE CHANGE in your life. Some change that will
help to create your world the way you want it to be. *Changing the Energy* around and within you, so that you can be

115

living your life the way you want to, isn't as difficult as you might imagine. With a little bit of creativity, it can be used as a major tool for turning an ordinary woman's life into an *Extraordinary* one!

My good friend M.J. is a graphic artist who often helps out at the local hospital, aiding and assisting very ill people. She told me that when she is working with these people her goal is to lift their spirits and help them to change the negative energy that is often around them due to their illnesses. M.J. shared with me a tool that she learned a long time ago in a friend's workshop that she swears works every time!

Initially, she lets the person vent for a while. She's learned that sometimes that's all that's necessary for someone to feel better. But if it continues, she gently asks them, *"What is the best thing that has happened to you today?"* She said that almost instantly you can see in their eyes and on their faces a refocusing of their energy.

When I asked her to give me an example of how this works, MJ went on to tell me about the time she was driving through Mexico with our friend Ginny, when suddenly they were pulled over by a "testosterone macho, pumped cop." He had stopped them for driving with the wrong numbered license plate for that day, which of course they didn't know about, since this was the first time they had heard about it as they were just passing through.

After the policeman had been ranting and raving for about 20 minutes, waving the threat of their car being towed and a $200.00 fine, M.J. turned to him and said, *"So tell me, what is the best thing that happened to you today?"*

He stopped for a minute, obviously a bit taken back by such a question under the circumstances, and then said, "Well, just one hour ago I had to stop a man whose car was weaving down the street who also had the wrong plates on. As I was about to give him a ticket, the poor man broke down crying and said that he was on his way to the hospital because he had just gotten a call that his brother had died." The officer went on to say that he felt really good about comforting him and letting him go without a ticket, and *that was the best thing that happened to him that day!*

She said that as she and Ginny watched him telling them his story, his entire body language changed and his demeanor softened. Not only did he *not* give them a fine or tow them away, he escorted them out of town, complete with sirens and flashing lights!

M.J. went on to say, "When you ask someone *'what is the best thing that happened to you today?'* or any other unexpected pleasant question, you give the other person an opportunity to change the focus of their thoughts, which then *Changes the Energy.* With just a few words you can turn two unlike strangers into just two likeable human beings."

After M.J. shared this gem with me, I went around testing my own variation of her line, and she was right! At first some people bristled a bit or looked at me strangely, but the longer I stayed with my open and positive attitude, the softer the other person got. It doesn't take me very long to detect a little smile in their eyes as they secretly welcome the opportunity to get out of their negative mood. A place that at one time or another each of us tends to get stuck in, and for whatever reason just can't seem to get out of ourselves, even when we want to.

One thing an ordinary woman who is having an *Ex*traordinary life learns, is that it is definitely a moment to moment thing. An action taken in one moment becomes attached to another action or response in the next moment, and because of that things can go either way.

Your job is to be consciously aware of these moments, and to always be on the lookout for the opportunity to affect *POSITIVE CHANGE* in your life as well as in the lives of others. When you can create your own set of tools for *Changing The Energy* into a positive heart energy that allows you to work better with less stress and strain, you can more effectively allow yourself to better apply your talents and strengths.

Creating what's called "active energy," an energy that is produced by motion and movement, can not only change your mood but can also improve your metabolism. When your metabolism is working harder you naturally turn up your ability to burn off excess fat and toxic waste, which makes you healthier during stressful times. Now that's what I call a win-win!

Making a *POSITIVE CHANGE* by positively *Changing The Heart Energy* that is around you, is an excellent way to change any ordinary woman's life into an *E*xtraordinary one!

Seven Tips for Creating Positive Heart Energy...

1. **Find ways to manage your challenges.** Everyone feels down at times, over-whelmed, confused and frustrated. Positive heart energy is a good change.

2. **Confide in those you trust** with your fears, hopes and mistakes. It's one of the best ways to improve your mind-body health, and to create positive energy.

3. **Write it down and then let it go.** Get those nasty feelings out of your body onto paper. It frees up your positive heart energy to create change.

4. **Appreciate and acknowledge others.** Any time you validate, compliment or appreciate another, you create a heartfelt energetic positive effect.

5. **Ask "why not?"** rather than "why." None of us knows for sure what's going to happen, so why not go for it? Positive energy creates courage for risks.

6. **Find the work you were born to do.** When you can actively pursue your passion, your positive change and heartfelt energy creates enthusiasm and joy.

7. **Love it or leave it.** Doing anything and being with anyone that closes your heart is an energy sapper. Positive change and heartfelt energy is where it's at!

CHAPTER 24

Self-Respect

Teach People How You Want to Be Treated

"Ok Joy, I need some advice," was how Cherie said hello to me on Monday morning. "John just left a message on my answering machine telling me how sorry he was that he never got back to me last weekend. He said that he had gotten totally bogged down with some business responsibilities."

"So what's the question?" I asked.

"Well I don't like it when someone says they're going to call me to get together and then they don't. It makes me feel as if I don't even matter enough to them to do what they say they are going to do. So the question is, should I or shouldn't I call him back, or should I just wait until he calls again? And if I do call him back, what should I say to him?"

Interestingly, my conversation with Cherie was just a variation of the one I had with my daughter the day before about a friend who had been caught gossiping about something she had told her in the strictest of confidence. As well as the one I had last week with Dana about Joe, who keeps making dates with her and then calls her at the last minute to change the time or the day.

These may seem like different stories but they all have the same theme. Someone is upset with someone else because of the way they are being treated, and their sense of their own *Self-Respect* leaves them confused about what to do. And why does this scenario happen again and again to so many of us? Because most of us aren't doing anything to change it!

I know this one only too well, because for years I would continuously stuff my feelings of discontent down inside. I hated confrontations and my constant stomach pains were living proof of that. Even though I know *intellectually* that no one is a mind reader and we all have different ways of doing things, I still assumed that other people *would just know* or do what I considered the right thing to do. And when they didn't respond exactly as I expected or wanted them to, I would get upset or at the very least, feel hurt or diminished. I definitely was in need of bolstering my *SELF-RESPECT* like a lot of other women, but didn't know exactly how to begin. But as they say, "when the student is ready the teacher will appear."

Dale is one of those wonderfully bright, evolved, generous of spirit and fiercely independent women. She has spent many years working on herself and has learned to live life by her own rules. We had initially met through our mutual friend, Lily, who most of the time was the one who orchestrated all of us getting together. So it wasn't until Lily and Ed moved to Iowa that Dale and I actually had a chance to create our own one-on-one relationship.

One of the things that really matters to me in relationship with my friends, is that they respect me enough to return my phone calls within a day or two. My philosophy is that you can always find the time to do the things that you want to do. When someone can't find a minute to return my call, it makes me feel as though I can't be very important to them.

I don't really care if a message is left on my answering machine or the returned call says, "Sorry sweetie, but I can't really talk to you now, my dog is having kittens." It's the gesture that counts. So needless to say it used to really annoy me when I would call Dale and days would go by without her returning my call. One day when we were out to lunch and talking about one thing or another, my not so hidden underlying feelings came seeping out into our conversation. Finally she turned to me and said, "Joy, what's going on with you today? You are not your *Joy*ous self."

Well, I guess that was all I needed for my heart to break open and for the words to come pouring out in the form of my upset and thwarted expectations. What was so interesting is that when I finished, she didn't apologize but instead she gave me a life changing present.

She looked at me in wide-eyed disbelief and said, "Why didn't you say something to me sooner? Haven't you learned yet that you need *To Teach People How You Want To Be Treated?* If no one ever says to another person, 'This is how I want to be treated or this kind of behavior is not acceptable to me and I need to be treated differently,' why would anyone change a behavior that is clearly very acceptable to them?

When you ask someone to alter the way they treat you, you are not only taking control over satisfying your own needs, but you are showing yourself and others the *Respect* you have for your *Self*. And best of all, you are giving the other person a chance to show you just how much you really mean to them.

When people don't return my call I just assume they're busy and will call when they can. But if that's not how you feel, and it really matters to you that your friends call you back within a certain amount of time, then you know what girlfriend? It will be my pleasure to honor your wish!"

Another thing that Dale taught me, which is the best part of this age-old wisdom, is that by *Teaching People How You Want To Be Treated* you are giving them one of the greatest gifts you ever could, the tools and the knowledge of how to be *the best* friend, family member, partner or co-worker that they can be…for you. It's another opportunity for each of us to show up in the world as the quality person we always want to be.

Building up your own reservoir of experiences that helps to reinforce your *Self-Respect* is a bit by bit, moment to moment experience, like most other things. Relationships that give you joy and happiness by being positive and satisfying certainly help to fill up the space.

If you are like me, and have certain expectations that need to be realized before you can feel good about yourself and the relationships you have with other people, it's *up to you* to make sure that the people in your life know what they are. Without this information people are only capable of doing what they have always done before, and *it's you* who is not giving them the opportunity to change. When you take the time to *Teach People How You Want To Be Treated*, you're also saying that this relationship matters to me, and I am willing to take the chance of losing it at the cost of making it better.

Your statement to the world and to yourself is, "I have such a great amount of *Self-Respect*, and I am only willing to accept the kind of treatment I deserve and that I will give in return." Learn to *Teach People How You Want To Be Treated*, and *E*xtraordinary relationships will be what you will receive in return.

Seven Tips for Enhancing Your Self-Respect...

1. **You teach others how to treat you.** It's up to you to show others what is acceptable to you, what your standards and boundaries are. What you need.

2. **Don't expect more than you're willing to give.** Don't expect to get without having to give in return. Show respect for others and others will respect you.

3. **Love yourself first.** Relationships mirror each other's actions and reactions. You can only receive as much respect as you are willing to give yourself.

4. **Know thine own self.** Know what it is that you really want and need. Ask for it without apologies or manipulating others. Listen to what others need.

5. **Take care of your own needs first.** Others want to give you more when it's their choice to give you what you want, not just because you are needy.

6. **Find out and give others what they need,** not what you want or think they need. Give to others as you would want others to give to you in return.

7. **Don't sell yourself short or play small.** There is no benefit to anyone when you diminish your self-respect or needs. Stand tall and play full out.

CHAPTER 25

Self-Worth

Walk Your Talk

I have come to believe that there is a time in each woman's life when she crosses some invisible line between "acting as if" and becoming her authentic self. It has nothing to do with how much style you have or business expertise you have accumulated or even how mature you might be. It is one of those indescribable delicious moments in time when you *know* that without a doubt, or without any need to have any other person affirm you, the face you are presenting to the world and your convictions, values, and true beliefs have finally all meshed together into one glorious example of womanhood. At that precise moment if anyone would ask you, "Who do you think you are?" Your enthusiastic reply would have to be, "This is who I am!"

In a world where men have been taught since boyhood to stand tall and shout from the rooftops all of their accomplishments and merits, women have been taught to play it small; be humble, act according to what's proper and acceptable, play the game. Sadly, it's not just men who are keeping this long outdated form of behavior alive, many women support it as well. It's OK to do "a little bit better" than your girlfriend, maybe lose a little bit of weight before she has, get a little higher up on the career ladder, even meet a love interest. But unfortunately when we really get on that train to success and it's not stopping for anything, many of our friends just can't handle it.

We have been taught to share our suffering and share our pain; in fact this is the way most women bond. But when the time comes to get past sharing our wounds and then finally move onto recovery, and God willing, on to success and a new life, few women are prepared to share that with their friends. Oftentimes our first reaction is to defend it, pretend that it's no big thing, or to even belittle all the effort that we've put forth as we were working so hard to create this new life that we have always wanted. What is that all about?

Marianne Williamson wrote a wonderful poem that Nelson Mandela used in his inaugural speech. It says, "Our deepest fear is not that we are inadequate. Our deepest fear is that we are powerful beyond measure. It is our light, not our darkness, that most frightens us. We ask ourselves, who am I to be brilliant, gorgeous, talented and fabulous? Actually who are you not to be? We don't serve anyone by playing small and when we let our own light shine, we unconsciously give others permission to do the same."

When you acknowledge your own *SELF-WORTH* and agree to always *Walk Your Talk*, every part of you is on the line. There's no room for fudging, dodging, weaving, or any other action that doesn't move you in a straight forward line. "This is who I am," is a statement that takes full responsibility for all your accomplishments, mistakes, actions and experiences; the good and the bad.

When you honor your own value system and live your life with integrity and consideration for yourself and others, it shouts to the world, "This woman respects her own *Self-Worth*, and clearly is *Walking Her Talk*." It says, "This is who I am and I am proud of it! You can believe that what you see is what you get, and you can trust that my word and my actions are an expression of my true authentic self."

Be who you are, then do what you need to do, in order to get what you want. When you are being your true authentic self, others know it and respond with respect. There is nothing that is more freeing or more fun than being your authentic self, and nothing makes an ordinary woman's life more *Extraordinary* than honoring your own *Self-Worth* and then *Walk Your Talk!*

Seven Tips for Increasing Your Self-Worth...

1. **Make a promise to always be true to yourself.** When you honor your own wishes and needs first, then you never have to feel used or abused.

2. **Recognize your uniqueness.** Never forget that there is no one like you, so honor your differences. You are a rare and special jewel. Treasure that.

3. **Always express yourself in the way you want to.** Your opinions matters and your style is your own. Your ways are special to you and worth expressing.

4. **Learn how to support yourself.** Give yourself the gift of faith, courage and the confidence to be who you are and who you want to be...you're worth it!

5. **Learn to see yourself clearly,** through your own honest loving eyes. You can't be all things to all people, so find out who you are and then be true to it.

6. **Know your worth and value.** Never judge yourself by someone else's standards or expectations. Your personal worth is what you determine it to be.

7. **Honor who you are** rather than what others have defined you as. Let go of the outdated need to please others to be accepted—you already are the best!

CHAPTER 26

Self-Esteem

Beating Rejection

I don't think that there is a woman in this world who at one time or another hasn't experienced the bitter taste of rejection. Something or someone has made you feel as though you weren't worthy or acceptable enough to have something that they have that you want. And the more important the object of desire is to you, the more vulnerable you are to other people's opinions and behavior. Especially if you feel that their word is the law, so to speak.

But because rejection is so much a part of all our lives, most of us go out into the world with our chins jutted out, with a naïve assurance that our bravado will deflect any and all obstacles. We are convinced that we have learned how to play the game of life so well, we are truly crushed when the universe says "NO, or at least not now."

I certainly felt that way when I took my book to Joelle Delbourgo, my literary agent. I knew that I had really worked hard in recreating my private journal into a special book for women, and even though I was excited beyond belief when the first editor she submitted it to loved it and wanted to publish it, I wasn't shocked.

Thank goodness *I* wasn't going to have to endure the same torturous road of rejection so many New York Times Best Seller authors before me had. You know those writers who tell their story of how they had received thirty or thirty-five rejections of their books before someone agreed to publish their book. Then they went on to become famous around the world, as their books went on to sell millions.

I just assumed those in power in the publishing world would be savvy enough to get my book immediately, and the rest would be history. Imagine my disappointment and surprise when my agent called to tell me "how upset the editor was because the marketing division of her company wouldn't give her the go ahead to publish my book. They felt that they weren't strong enough in the self-help divisions to do it justice." In one split second, I was a member of the elite group of potential best selling *rejected* authors!

So after I went through the "required amount of wallowing time" in my disappointment, I started to think about how often and how many different ways we all experience *Rejection* and why. I wondered, would I have felt those painful pangs that come with rejection if I had simply gone into the process of getting published expecting my fair share of rejections before I was accepted? Was my downfall thinking I would be one of the lucky ones, and that I wouldn't have to experience the same fate that so many before me had to endure? Or is rejection something we are all destined to experience, like some necessary evil we all need in order to grow? And if so, is there anything we can do about it?

Living on this earth for more than a few decades has taught me some very valuable lessons. One of the biggest ones is that we rarely learn anything of importance until we are hit on the head and taken down. Then we are forced to reach for something to hold onto, just so we can get back up and off of our knees.

Rarely do we change our way of thinking or way of being without something shaking us up a bit. It seems like only then do we find the courage to go deep within, to search for one thing that can protect us from almost anything, and that something is called SELF-ESTEEM.

Self-Esteem means having a deep sense of your own worth that gives you the same respect, generosity, kindness, love and consideration you would give to someone else for whom you really care for and respect. "It's the courage to accept yourself in spite of being unacceptable," as the philosopher Paul Tilliach once said.

As my greatest mentor and mom use to say, "It's fairly easy to get the things that might make you feel comfortable in this world, but until you discover your own worth and develop your own sense of Self-Esteem, there will always be a hole inside of you that all forms of poison can fall into. It's up to you to learn how to love yourself so completely, assigning to yourself a level of value and worth so great, that no one can ever destroy you or tear you down. Once you develop your own sense of bravery and self-authority, nothing can ever really harm you again."

So how do you develop this thing called Self-Esteem? Well, the good news is your level of Self-Esteem is up to you and the bad news is your Self-Esteem is up to you! It's up to you to find the courage to destroy those outdated tapes of "untruths" that tells you that you are less than perfect, and replace them with new tapes that reinforce the truth of your own magnificence.

Your work is to find that special place deep within where all the wisdom and knowledge that you were born with, and have accumulated in this lifetime, is there waiting for you to access. That all-knowing center that you go to when you need to be reminded that no one else in the entire universe is exactly like you, and just because of that, you will always be more than enough.

It's important to remember that when you feel rejected it's because you have given your power over to someone else. You have gone into agreement that someone else's opinion and the way they behave is an accurate statement of whether you are acceptable or not.

If you have ever felt rejected because some guy you met somewhere said he would call and then he didn't, it's because you gave him the power to judge whether or not you were acceptable enough to call. If you hadn't, then his saying he would call and then he doesn't, would be just one of those things jerks do. If some short sided person in the marketing department didn't have the smarts enough to want to publish my book, then it was up to me to turn that rejection into a win.

Once you have developed your own sense of *SELF-ESTEEM* you will use it continuously to guide and reinforce you. No one but you will ever again determine if you or anything you do is acceptable or not. You and you alone will be the judge of that, and *Beating Rejection* will be you way. Learning to have *esteem for yourself*, makes it a sure bet that your ordinary life will be *"esteemly"* $\mathcal{E}$xtraordinary!

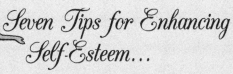

Seven Tips for Enhancing Self-Esteem...

1. **Do it anyway! Take risks! Let yourself feel success!** No one can make you feel worthy or successful but you. Do whatever you need to do to feel that way.

2. **The best you can do is notice what's happening.** It's ok to feel anxious, scared or lazy. As long as you don't let that stop you from moving forward.

3. **You need to have a purpose.** You need to know where you want to be, and what you need to get there. The process keeps you moving to who you want to be.

4. **Self-esteem takes introspection and comparisons.** Find your unique ways of being one of a kind. Compare your assets—learn to love and honor your gifts.

5. **Make a list of things that make you feel proud** of yourself. Make that list once a week. When you doubt your worth, bring out the list and read it.

6. **Discover you. Get to know the you worth loving.** Self-esteem comes from having great esteem for who you are, what you do and why you're special.

7. **Learn to accept the things that you can't change.** If it's your body, remember how it has served you. If you think you're not enough. Know that's a lie!

CHAPTER 27

Kindness

The Random Act That Changes Everything

One of the qualities that I have always admire when I see it in someone else is *KINDNESS*. A person who takes the time to be kind and considerate to each and every person that comes into their life. Someone that takes the time to be nice, no matter how important or busy they are.

This was instilled in me when I was an impressionable young girl and our family belonged to a rather ritzy country club. It was the kind of club where people often tried to show off their wealth and importance by barking orders at the help or walking around with their very important noses in the air. Because I was too young to understand why I felt so different from many of these people, I often times felt as if I didn't belong there; And then I met Mrs. Green.

Mrs. Green was an older very wealthy philanthropic woman, considered by many the doyenne of Philmont Country Club. A woman with such a presence and prestige you almost felt as if you should bow when she walked by. But if you had, she would have surely bent down to pick you up, since she was one of the kindest women I have ever known.

It didn't matter if you were a member of the staff or a member of the club, she would always go out of her way to stop for a moment to say a kind word or inquire how you were doing. I was just a kid, yet whenever she saw me she would always take the time to stop, say hello and chat for awhile.

Her way of treating everyone with equal kindness and consideration, no matter what their age or station in life, became my standard for how I have tried to treat people for most of my life. I have learned that most people just want to be seen and acknowledged. Because this is missing in so many people's lives, they behave in ways that could often be interpreted as selfish or even cruel. Yet the moment you show the slightest bit of tenderness, they change their demeanor almost instantly.

So now when I see myself getting upset with the rude and hurtful words people seem to vomit on each other, I personally focus on making a difference. Often it's by delivering some *Random Act of Kindness*, which helps to defuse some of the negativity that unfortunately seems to be running amuck in our world.

A compliment on an employee's work to their superior, a kind word to a frazzled waiter or waitress or a one minute call to let someone else know how much they mean to you. It could be an acknowledgment to someone close to you for a job well done or telling a friend or family member what joy they bring to your life. All of these simple and easy gestures can transform someone's negative day into a positive one, and can be just the *Random Act of Kindness* that they needed at that moment.

I have learned that the best any of us can do to positively change the world, is to concentrate our efforts on one person at a time. Instead of getting upset with the way people seem to insist on treating each other these days, try to practice channeling your energy into a totally opposite direction and watch how it *Changes Everything*!

When you can take just a moment to stop and evaluate what's really going on with someone else, and then ask yourself what does this person I am interacting with really want or need from me, you usually can give it to them and the world becomes a better place. More times than not, its just taking the time to show another person that you see them and that you care.

Often times people who are mean, rude, or cruel to other people just want attention, and this is how they go about getting it. It sort of reminds me of the little kid who causes trouble just so their mommy will notice them. I guess that's because most of us are only little kids in our grown-up bodies, and unfortunately some of those kids have been really abused. When you can take the time to respond to someone with *KINDNESS*, consideration, and a little attention, when you take the time to see "the God as well as the child within," something magical happens!

Last week I was asked to be the Toastmaster at my bimonthly Toastmaster's meeting, which by the way is a wonderful organization for anyone who wants to perfect their speaking skills. Because I had been out of the country for quite awhile I had forgotten what was expected of me. So I called Jane, one of the members, and asked her for advice.

She told me that all I had to do was to be a hostess, so to speak, which clearly I knew how to do. So I decided to have fun with this experience and to treat this evening as if I was entertaining dear friends at my home.

Before the meeting I went to the local market to pick up some fresh lemonade and chocolate chip cookies, because for me having delicious refreshments helps to make a great party. When I went to check-out my things I noticed that the check-out girl was being abrasive and almost nasty to the customer in front of me, a quality you know just warms my heart.

When it was my turn to checkout I started to get the same treatment; no surprise there. So I stepped back for a moment and asked myself what was really going on here. I noticed that with her curtness the girl was also doing a lot of sniffling. So I said to her, "Looks like you've got a nasty summer cold there. That must really be uncomfortable."

At first she seemed almost shocked and surprised that I was actually inquiring about her health, but with a weak smile she replied that it was her allergies. "What a bummer," I replied, "My mom seems to have the same problem and she tried this new product and maybe it would work for you."

For the next five minutes it took to check me out, we spoke of the pros and cons of the various possible cures and medicines that were out there for her to take. When it was time for me to leave I told her that I hoped she felt better. She turned to me with a huge smile and said,

"Thanks so much, you have already made me feel better!"

So with those good feeling inside of me I went to Toastmasters and proceeded to conduct the meeting as I had intended. I encouraged "my guests" to introduce themselves to each other, and when they stood-up to speak to tell us how they happen to come to the group, which is not typically done at the meetings. I then proceeded to invite them to partake in the refreshments I had brought and to sit back and enjoy the rest of the "party."

Because there are so many different personalities that come to these meetings, one never knows exactly what the reactions are to any of your speeches or actions. So when I went home that night, I wasn't really sure whether or not others had or had not approved of my maverick way of being a Toastmaster.

Before the next meeting began something compelled me to go over to say hello and welcome a woman whom I had sensed was shy and maybe even felt like a bit of an outsider. Well my instincts couldn't have been more right on, because she just lit up like a Christmas tree as I approached her.

"Hi Joy, oh I am so glad you came over to speak to me! I wanted to tell you how much I enjoyed the last Toastmasters meeting and how much it affected me. I often want to be more social and outgoing, but never really know what to do. When you went out of your way to make everyone feel so welcomed and a part of the group, and then made sure that everyone met everyone else as they shared their stories and your delicious refreshments, I felt as if you were doing it especially for me. Not only do I finally feel like I belong here, but you taught me how to make people feel comfortable. I am now going to start to invite lots of different people to my home and do exactly what you did! Thank you so much for your *KINDNESS*, it means so much to people like me."

So there it was, by simply doing a *Random Act of Kindness* because it felt like it was the right thing to do, I had actually changed a person's life beyond what I had ever imagine. It taught me once again that you never know how

141

your actions will change someone's life, and how important kind words and right action really are.

I certainly never went out that day with the intentions of changing someone's life by buying cookies and lemonade to host a meeting, but there it was and I had. By exercising A *Random Act Of Kindness* I had turned the moment of an ordinary woman's life into an *Extraordinary* one, and that's not even mentioning what it did for me!

KINDNESS is a wonderful gift to give yourself and everyone that comes into your life, and such an easy thing to do. Remember, A *Random Act of Kindness* has the power to *Change Everything*!

Seven Tips for Kindness That Changes Things...

1. **Take a minute and listen to what others say.** Oftentimes all anyone wants is to be listened to. Taking the time to listen can change everything.

2. **Do something totally thoughtful** and totally unexpected. Doing a random act of kindness can fill up a heart and soul like nothing else can.

3. **Be kind to your supposed enemies.** Nothing can change a negative situation into a positive one like love and sincere kindness.

4. **Treat the little people like the big people.** When you get into the habit op treating everyone the same, everyone feels equally good.

5. **Kindness is a way of life and an attitude.** It's true; what you put out you get back. If kindness is your way of life, life will be kind to you.

6. **Be as kind to yourself as you are to others.** Never forget that kindness starts at home. Spend today being kind to yourself.

7. **Random acts of kindness,** without a concern as to whether or not you are acknowledged for them, builds personal worth, value and self-esteem.

CHAPTER 28

Making a Difference

One Person at a Time

The times are changing and it's for the good. More and more women are concerned with MAKING A DIFFER-ENCE one of their top priorities. Looking for the ways and means to incorporate their careers, personal lives, inter-ests, and avocations into the service of helping others. But sometimes life just seems to get in the way, and a mild frus-tration sets in. Work is about work, family and friends are about responsibilities, and our obligations, hobbies and in-terests have just become a part of our time-consuming list.

With all that we have to do there is barely enough time to get *half* of what is required done, no less the time to be of service to others or include them in our worldly visions. So we walk around doing the best we can, harboring a secret fantasy of sitting next to Oprah helping her with her latest project to change the world, yet sadly assuming that it will probably have to be in another lifetime.

The idea of writing this book came out of my deep desire to share some of the revelations that have changed my life, and to show other women that it really is possible to have an easier and more joyful life. The idea of showing women how easy it is to change the quality of their lives by simply changing the way they choose to perceive the various circumstances of their life, really excited me.

As I began to put my list together of the issues I wanted to cover in the book, I realized that I would have to examine how I was dealing with each and every one of those issues. Was I really capable of teaching other ordinary women like myself how to have an *Extraordinary* life? More times than not I was left with the thought of "what difference could I possibly make?" I felt like I had so much more to learn myself. Would anyone really care about how an ordinary woman living in Connecticut (and Mexico) is having an *Extraordinary* life? More importantly, do all women really have the same issues?

One day after spending a long week of exhausting editing and reediting my book, I called my sweet friend Randi to vent my frustrations. After what must have seemed like forever, she lovingly said, "Are you done? Do you feel like you've said all you wanted to say on the subject?" Well to tell you the truth I probably could have gone on for another hour, but I said, "Yes, I am done."

"Good," she said, "because I have something to tell you. Since we have been friends I must have called you at least a hundred times with my various upsets and cries for help and advice. You were *always* there for me and *you always Make A Difference*. Every single time I called you, by the time I hang up, I always felt better and more in control of whatever problem or situation I was in. In fact, just thinking about what you would say, was enough to calm me down.

And then do you know what I would do? I would usually call my sister, or my girlfriends Barbara or Judy, and I would share with them the words of wisdom that you had just shared with me. They were always inspired by what you had said, and then tell me that they couldn't wait to share it with their friends. By the time your words of wisdom have done the circuit, I bet you have touched a thousand different hearts! Joy, you' re always MAKING A DIFFERENCE, you're just doing it One Person At A Time."

Well, if that wasn't the cat's meow. I've been sitting here wanting to be just like Oprah, who works pretty darn hard to Make A Difference in millions of people's lives, and all I needed to do was call Randi to have the same effect! The message was loud and clear. You may not have the audience of a national television host or the following of a some well-known author, lecturer or guru, but that doesn't mean that you can't make a difference to thousands of people, One Person At A Time. My friend Randi, the original Mother Earth, is a perfect example of that. Because you decided to buy this book and read this story, you are now being touched by Randi's supportive words to me. Words that now have the potential of Making a Difference in your life as well!

Because of this experience I now speak to everyone I meet with a different consciousness. Since you never know which words will touch someone's aching heart or be a transforming experience for them, it's important to be consciously aware of all your interactions. It could be just those few uplifting words that you give to a friend on the phone, or the advice you shared with the troubled woman at the gym, or that compliment you might give to the stranger with the pretty blue eyes.

You just never know the difference your words could be making, *One Person at a time*. One moment at a time, one person at a time, is the way of *Making a Difference* for turning an ordinary woman life into an $\mathscr{E}$xtraordinary life!

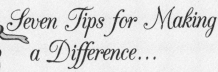

Seven Tips for Making a Difference...

1. **Always remember, it's quality not quantity.** If your actions are generated from a loving heart, just a few words at the right time can make a difference.

2. **Compassion is what people need more than anything.** Really listening to someone's problems and concerns, can be all that they need to know someone cares.

3. **Go that extra mile when someone is in need.** By taking the time to call, write, email or go visit, just your efforts can be enough to make a difference.

4. **Show others who they really are.** When you can be a mirror reflection of another's perfection, you give them the opportunity to see their best side.

5. **Speak to someone's higher self,** instead of their past performances or historical behavior. Give others the chance to do better or even change.

6. **Keep a secret.** When people know that they can tell you something really private and it won't go any further, it frees them up to tell their truth.

7. **You can make a difference** when you give up how it looks to others, or how important what you are doing is. Care about others and you can change the world.

CHAPTER 29

Joy

The Peak Experience

"Joy to the world and the fishes in the deep blue sea, Joy to you and me," (or some version of that song) has been a part of my intro for a long time now whenever someone asks me to repeat my name. It always seems like a bit more fun than just merely repeating my name or going into a monologue on what the word JOY means, (which is really what I want to do!) You see as crazy as it may seem, I believe that a person has some sort of responsibility to live *Joyfully* when one has a name like *Joy*. And even though I know that there isn't really any one thing that can give someone a guaranteed *Extraordinary* life, what I do know is that the absence of deeply felt *Joy* will pretty much guarantee you a life far less than spectacular.

JOY, the source of great pleasure or delight, is one of the highest of human elations one can experience. It goes way beyond happiness and is much bigger than any emotional response you could ever have when you experience some good luck, see your hard work finally paying off, or feel a sense of relief from your daily stress or anxiety. It's a quality of thought that infuses your mind, body, and spirit with a sense of personal power, inner wisdom, and mental clarity. It stimulates your immune system, increases your energy, and helps you stretch beyond any previously assumed boundaries.

It opens your heart, keeps you centered in the midst of your difficulties, and heightens your ability to tap into your unlimited creativity. This amazing state of mind manifests itself in your daily life in just a heartbeat, as more freedom, acceptance, compassion, excitement, enthusiasm, passion, love, pleasure, and harmony. Pretty incredible this feeling called *Joy* don't you think?

But as crazy as it may seem there are actually some women who are afraid to be *too* positive, *too* successful or have *too much Joy* in their lives. They know intellectually that life is to be enjoyed but have unfortunately chosen to believe, at some deep level, that they don't deserve that much of a good thing. Mentally and verbally they have agreed to live a life of continuous self-fulfilling prophecies that includes a lot of difficulties and misfortunes, instead of choosing to envision living a life that is easier and more *Joy*-filled.

If that's not bad enough when these women do have the good fortune of experiencing *Joy*, they are convinced that if they think about it or dare to verbalize aloud about how much happiness they are actually having in their lives, they will put a kinaherah (which is the Jewish word for maloykei which is the Italian word for mala suerte—which is the Spanish word for putting a jinx or a curse of bad luck) on themselves for speaking too much about a good thing and believing that *somehow* it will be taken away!

One of my heroes is Dr. Abraham Maslow, the creator of Human Potential Psychology. His work included the studies of men and women who were functioning as happy, healthy, successful people. His goal was to find out what these people were specifically doing that made their lives work so well. This was quite the opposite of many other studies being done at that time that were focusing on why so many people are unhappy and feel like failures.

He discovered that the majority of the people he studied in the midst of a difficult time, had the ability to return in their minds to various moments of "*Peak Experiences.*" Moments when they could vividly remember feeling totally exhilarated by life, loved the flow of creative expressions they were having, and enjoyed the enthusiasm they felt for something they had done or had the pleasure of experiencing. By returning in their minds to a time when they recognized their value and purpose for being here on earth, they could empower themselves to deal with the rough times and make themselves feel healthier and happier.

Dr. Maslow's studies opened the door to acknowledging the powerful connection between people who were living a *Joy*-filled life, and people who had the ability to remember and stay focused on seeing the positive and rewarding qualities of their lives. He called these people *actualized men and women*. *Actualized* meaning to make actual or real in the present moment.

These actualized individuals had the ability to return in their minds to the sensation they felt when they were having a *Peak Experience*. Then to use these feelings of Joy, enthusiasm, and exuberance as a stimulus to create easier and more *Joy*-filled moments at the present time. The had the ability to change the quality of their life.

Forged with this knowledge I began the process of recalling moments in my life that I felt were *Peak Experiences* so I could create my own positive memory bank. Once I started this process of recalling positive moments, it surprised me to see how many heightened experiences I had to draw from, which was quite a change from say 20 years ago.

"How did that happen?" I asked myself. "What did I do to shift my experience of life from half-empty to half-full?" The answer that kept rising to the top of the list was recalling the day I decided to make having the experience of JOY my highest and most important commitment. I had made the decision that no matter what was going on in my life, if something didn't feel right in my mind or body, I would make myself stop what I was doing, and look at what was really going on.

I would begin asking myself questions. "Is what's happening in your life right now making you feel *Joyful*, and if not, why not? Is there anything that you can personally do right now to bring more *Joy* into your life, and if so, what?"

If experiencing JOY is your highest commitment, then *everything* needs to bring you some form of *Joy*, even if it's only being aware that in the worst of times, there is a gift in learning another one of life's never ending lessons. If you are not experiencing some form of *Joy* then you need to look at what you are doing, who you are doing it with, and why you are doing it. Once you make having *Joy* your highest and most important commitment, It becomes increasingly difficult for you to stay with any one upset for very long.

And if the circumstances and recent events of your life are filled with pain and suffering and there are things that have happened that no amount of *Joyful* thinking is ever going to change, then now more than ever remembering the good times can be just the thing to help move the healing process along.

It's not that I am suggesting that having a commitment to *Joy* can take away the initial hurt, pain, sadness, upset, or disappointments that life sometimes throws our way. Nor that my commitment to *Joy* will somehow affect my forever childlike wishful thinking that one day it will. But what I have noticed is that when you can refocus your thoughts even for just a little while, life seem just a little bit more bearable.

I have also noticed that I can "get off of it" sooner, start looking for the learning lesson in the painful experience sooner, find my way to include it all and get back to living a lot sooner. When I allow *Joy* back into my my life things just natural shift.

One great way to accelerate the process is to make a list of all the things in your life that have brought you *Joy* this week, this month, this year. Try to add to this list periodically and put it some place where you can see it daily. I have found that having gratitude for all your blessings is a wonderful way to help bring the feeling of *Joy* into your life. When you open your mind, your heart, and your spirit to recalling your *Peak Experiences*, you are also acknowledging and appreciating all of the wonderful times you have had in your life.

I know that I am a little prejudiced to the word JOY, but I truly can't think of any other emotion that has the power to turn an ordinary woman's life into an *Extraordinary* one quite like *Joy* can. When you take the time to see the *Extraordinary* in the ordinary, you will actually create more *Joy* in your life, and the ordinary will become *Extraordinary*! When you take a few minutes to occasionally stop and ponder all the *Peak Experiences* you've had in your life, you might be quite surprised at just how blessed you are, and what a *Joy* that will be!

Seven Tips for Joy to Be Your Peak Experience...

1. **Make JOY a priority in your life.** Look for anything and everything that can bring you happiness and JOY. If you're not joyful, change what you're doing.

2. **Never confuse a lack of JOY** with lack of money, what you have or don't have, or who you are. JOY is always within you and always within your reach.

3. **JOY is the most direct connection,** in the deepest way, to your spiritual self. It strengthen your sense of appreciation and gratitude for all of life.

4. **Become aware that JOY is always a choice.** In every moment you have the opportunity to choose JOY as your highest commitment—your way of life.

5. **JOY and love go hand and hand.** Find the piece in everyone and everything that you can love and enjoy. Learn to joyfully love it all, now and forever.

6. **When you use JOY as your source of strength,** and inspiration, you experience more love, happiness, prosperity, contentment and peace in your life.

7. **Say yes to JOY.** A yes that makes the earth shake and the walls tremble. Scream "yes" to it all! Yes, I am ready for a life of technicolor JOY!

Ending Thoughts

I imagine by now you have gotten the idea that the way an ordinary woman can have an Extraordinary life isn't about what she's got, but how she chooses to perceive what she's got. It certainly isn't about how much money, beauty, fame or fortune you have. What you do for a living or with whom you decide to share your life with. It's really all about how you choose to think, speak, act and react to the various circumstances of your life. And of course, if you truly believe that you deserve to have whatever it is you really want and need.

That's the simple secret of *How an Ordinary Woman Can Have an Extraordinary Life*; it all begins with a thought! The quality of your thoughts determines the quality of your life. The idea is so simple, yet so hard for so many people to actualize. With all my heart, I hope that this book has opened up your mind and heart to that thought. And since everything begins with a thought, then nothing could be more perfect than ending this book with a few of my own thoughts on *The Formula for the Art of Living Well*.

As you've seen, *The Formula For The Art of Living Well*, is not about going out and buying something or remaking yourself. It's all about understanding and utilizing your own personal power that begins and ends in your mind. What I love the most about the collection of vignettes that you've just read, is that they reinforce some of the most important life lessons anyone would ever need to know. Lessons that come in the form of messages that touch your heart as they make you stop and think about them in different ways that you might have thought about them before.

Fortified with an understanding of how *The Formula* works, and with these new thoughts inside your head, you can now see solutions where you once saw problems, joy where you once saw pain. *The Formula* becomes the way. Your way for how an ordinary woman can have an *Ex*traordinary life.

I have been working on my personal growth for many years now. The journey hasn't always been easy, but it certainly was a trip! Whenever I would became frustrated over not knowing what to do about one thing or another, I would reach for my private collection of stories and tips, and always there would be my answer.

The words and the messages of the stories always turned me around. Often times I felt as if I had returned to the loving arms of a dear sweet friend. Someone who cared enough to nudge me off my position, so that I could begin to live life just a little bit bigger and better than I might have been just a moment before. A gentle reminder of an inner knowing that we all have, but somewhere between the morning cup of coffee and brushing my teeth at night, it somehow was forgotten.

The Formula is not a new idea; it is how men and women have been creating their reality since the beginning of time. It is the process we each use for creating the quality of our lives, positively or negatively. But it wasn't until I had my moment of revelation, and then applied it in retrospect to all the various experiences of my life, that I truly understood its real power in creating my own Heaven or hell on earth.

For the first time after living a large part of my lifetime I understood what it really meant to take responsibility for your life. Finally I was capable of acknowledging how my own personal power and energy had affected the very best of times, and the very worst of times in my life. And once I was willing to own it all, came an even greater power. The power to truly create an *Ɛ*xtraordinary life.

The Formula is the way and the stories and tips in this book can be used as your support system time and time again, to create magic for you as you travel on through the days of your life. It's for all women who are living and loving much of their ordinary lives, yet in their hearts know that there is more to have, and want to take their lives to another level.

Understanding and properly utilizing the messages in *How an Ordinary Woman Can Have an Ɛxtraordinary Life* can truly change your life in ways you have only dreamed of. All it really takes is the desire and belief that you deserve to have the best of what life can offer you. Having the desire and willingness to own and do what it takes to have control over your own thoughts and behavior is a big part of having a better life. I promise you, once you get this one, nothing in your life will ever be the same!

Enjoy the journey! My thoughts will be with you.

Joy Weston is just an ordinary woman who *is having* an *E*xtraordinary life. And even though she's been a nationally recognized photographer and the co-creator of a natural skincare line of products, she feels that her most important credentials are in the example of the life she is now living.

Joy is the mother of two fabulous kids, a proud grandmother of two gorgeous munchkins and the wife of a terrific guy. She and her husband split their time between their homes in Connecticut and Mexico, and spend as much time as they can traveling and enjoying the world.

Joy is now in the process of producing her next book called *How an Ordinary Relationship Can Become an Extraordinary One: The Formula for the Art of Loving Well!* If you have a story and you are interested in being one of "the girls or guys" who shares their moment of transformation with Joy's readers in this upcoming book, please send it to the address below! And if you are interested in having her give a lecture or creating a workshop for your group, she would love to hear from you.

JOY WESTON
P.O. Box 2508
Westport, CT 06880
www.JoyWeston.com
joy@joyweston.com

The Seven "Must Haves" for Turning an Ordinary Life Into an Extraordinary One!

1. **A sense of joy and happiness** about your life, even when things aren't going the way you would like. Knowing that every lesson is a gift for your growth.

2. **A sense of love** for yourself, others and the world you live in, can heal, transform, and create miracles you never ever thought possible. Love cures all.

3. **A sense of abundance** that has nothing to do with how much money or material possessions you have, but a knowing of your universal never ending supply.

4. **A sense of self-worth** that recognizes your true value and reinforces your own self-esteem. An unshakable respect and belief in who you are.

5. **A sense of good health** that starts with a mind-body-spirit connection and then carries through to a commitment to diet, exercise and heart work.

6. **A sense of gratitude** that never let's you forget how blessed you really are. An appreciation for all the gifts and assistance that never stops coming.

7. **A sense of making a difference** with your family and friends, associates and strangers. Living a life of doing thoughtful and random acts of kindness.

Seven Tips for Becoming More Aware...

1. **Always be aware of what you are thinking.** The thoughts you focus on will create your life. Look at your life, and you'll know what you are thinking.

2. **Always be aware of what you are saying.** Your words are a reflection of what you are thinking. If they're not positive and supportive, change them.

3. **Always be aware that action reflects thought.** If you like or don't like the way you are acting or reacting...take a look at how you are thinking.

4. **Always be aware of how you believe.** If you believe you deserve to have what you really want, you'll eventually get it—if you don't—you won't.

5. **Always be aware that having an *Extraordinary* life**, begins with a thought and a commitment that comes from wanting the best life can offer you.

6. **Always be aware of your intentions** and let them be your guiding light. Intend to have the life you truly want and then be aware of what your intentions manifest.

7. **Always be aware of your choices.** The choices you make moment to moment create the threads that compose the tapestry of your life. Your choices will color your life.

Seven Tips for Forgiving and Not Blaming...

1. **Stay centered in the here and now.** Stop the action, count to ten and give yourself the time and space to disconnect from your upset.

2. **Take responsibility for your own feelings.** They are caused by your beliefs and life experiences. Become response-able, not reactive to words.

3. **Look for the lessons in all your experiences.** What about this experience is familiar? What can you learn from it? What can you do for a different outcome?

4. **Look at the risk you are taking.** Every time you go into the "blame game" you take the risk of damaging your relationships. Is that what you want to do?

5. **Playing the blame game** only prevents you from seeing your part in the upset. It holds you back from moving forward to a place of forgiveness—let it go.

6. **Open your heart and mind.** When your heart and mind are closed, nothing positive can come in. Keep them open for love and forgiveness and see what happens.

7. **Be grateful.** Count to ten and remember all the reasons you are grateful to have this person in your life. It's hard to be angry while feeling grateful.

Seven Tips for Better Communication...

1. **Take responsibility for the other person's listening.** If you don't feel as if you are being understood, try again. Say it in a different way until you are heard.

2. **Take responsibility for what you've heard.** Don't be attached to the words or what you think they mean. Ask for clarity and repeat back your interpretation.

3. **Take responsibility for what you want to express** and what you want from the situation. Take a moment to be clear with your thoughts and then your words.

4. **Align your values and intentions with your actions.** When you live your life from your sense of integrity, you don't have to fear any honest communication.

5. **Listen to the silence as much as the words.** We learn as much about others from the topics people aren't willing to talk about, as from what they are.

6. **Be as open to the criticism as to the validation.** Oftentimes we learn more about ourselves and others from the criticisms, than from the compliments given.

7. **Be flexible and willing to re-think and re-group.** If in the middle of a discussion you realize your position has changed, be woman enough to say so.

Seven Tips for Creating More Self-Confidence...

1. **Your level of self-confidence is up to you.** Change your perception of yourself and you will change your life. Choose to see your own magnificence.

2. **Be your own voice of self-affirmation.** Give yourself all of the compliments and acknowledgment you wish others had or could possibly give to you.

3. **Surround yourself with people who appreciate who you are.** Self-confidence is reinforced when others reflect your own glorious light right back to you.

4. **Give to yourself as you give unto others you love.** Be generous with respect and a deep caring for all that you are. It builds a strong self-confidence.

5. **Self-confidence is about trusting your own heart** and acknowledging your own personal wisdom. You know what's best for you because you are the best!

6. **Self-confidence comes from within.** Make working on your personal growth the most important thing, and you will learn to trust your own knowing self.

7. **Love yourself first and everything else falls into place.** Define the world in your own terms and then sit back and enjoy the accolades and applause.

Seven Tips for Letting Go of Suffering...

1. **Use your mind over the matter.** No matter what it looks or feels like, if you choose to think things will be better, sooner than later they will be.

2. **Learn to smile from the inside out**, smiling changes you mentally and physically. Put a smile on your face and the struggles hold a lot less power.

3. **Change your actions and reactions.** If you keep on doing the same things you'll keep on getting the same results. Positive actions get positive results.

4. **Think how you want to be.** Give up the struggle and suffering by seeing yourself as happy, successful living an abundant life. Fake it till you make it!

5. **If necessary, alter your world.** If where you are and the people in your life are bringing you down, change the people or change your viewpoint.

6. **Help others and you help yourself.** When you take the time to help others in need your problems seem to fade into the background. Caring feels good.

7. **Create your own support system.** Read magazine articles, books, listen to tapes, talk to friends. Find your own source of constant encouragement.

Seven Tips for a Better Body Image...

1. **Begin today practicing sweet talk.** Instead of telling yourself all the things that are wrong, try seeing and saying nice things to yourself.

2. **Beauty is in the eyes of the beholder.** No one size or shape pleases everyone. Try seeing your body through the eyes of the beholder who likes it.

3. **Look at the clothes you always feel good in.** Now repeat them in every possible combination. Accentuate the positive and eliminate the negative.

4. **Concentrate on the area above the neck.** Put a smile on your face, a twinkle in your eye and add an interested and interesting mind—they'll love ya!

5. **Your body is your temple**...take good care of it. Respect it—mentally, physically, emotionally and spiritually. Worship yourself; You're worth it.

6. **Create your own program for good health.** No matter what you've got—without your health— you've got nothing. Make it an important priority.

7. **Learn to be "bien dans sa peau,"** comfortable in your own skin. When others see that you are okay with your body, they will respond accordingly.

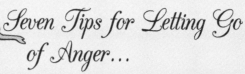

Seven Tips for Letting Go of Anger...

1. **Give up vomiting out hurtful words** based on problems or mistakes made in the past. Invisible hurtful scars remain long after the fight is over.

2. **Keep your arguing to yourselves.** Keep it private and don't involve outsiders. Don't gather judges in your defense or create gossip for later on.

3. **Stick to the subject.** Don't confuse the issue with things that can only diffuse the importance of what really matters. Stay with what's going on now.

4. **Don't throw threats into your fight** that you don't really want to carry out. This is dirty fighting and can cause serious backlash and added upsets.

5. **Keep it real.** Don't waste precious time hiding behind safe topics that prevent you from owning up to what's really bothering you. Honesty pays off.

6. **Steer your conversation towards finding a solution.** Speak to the other person's higher self. Help them understand with the intentions for this to be a win-win.

7. **Be a gracious winner**—remember, in a relationship there's no such thing as neutral—you either build it up or destroy it through your actions.

Seven Tips for Aging With Style...

1. **How you see yourself is more important** than how others see you. "Youthful" is a very personal thing. Age is truly just a number and a mind set.

2. **Don't buy into what others say is appropriate** for your age. Go where you want, do what you want, and dress the way you want. It's your life, enjoy it!

3. **See the changes in your appearance objectively**, not in the harsh light of age comparison. You just might discover a more beautiful and youthful you!

4. **Focus in on what is your best look** for this time of your life. Choose carefully and buy the best quality items you can afford. Make your own statement.

5. **Do things that make you feel beautiful.** Dress up or dress down. Laugh, sing, dance, go to parties, give parties. Do whatever, just do it with panache!

6. **Keeping your mind and body healthy and active** is vital for eternal youth. A fit body, sparkling eyes and an inquisitive mind are irresistible to everyone.

7. **Stay true to yourself and your own unique style.** The most beautiful women are the ones who don't submit to any standard of beauty. They define it.

Seven Tips for Increasing Your Happiness…

1. **Allow yourself the gift of feeling worthy** and deserving enough to have all the happiness and joy that are a part of your natural birthright!

2. **Immerse yourself in the good times today.** Don't let the fears of the bad times take away from your potential happiness today—live in the moment!

3. **Fill yourself up with memories of happy times.** Let them be your strength and support to handle the many challenges that will come your way!

4. **Follow your bliss**—once a day do something that makes you feel happy and happy to be alive. Find your passions and then fully enjoy them!

5. **Do something worthwhile.** Experience being fully engaged in doing whatever gives you purpose and makes you feel worthwhile…and be happy!

6. **Make someone happy.** Do something special for a loved one, compliment a stranger, say a kind word. Their happiness will bounce right back at you!

7. **Choose to be happy,** choose to make happiness a constant part of your life, anyone can. It's as easy as saying "happiness is a constant part of my life!"

Seven Tips for Encouraging Personal Growth...

1. **Free yourself from living by other people's rules.** This is your life. Do what you want with it and be consciously aware of the life you are creating.

2. **View every experience as a gift for your growth.** The best of times and the worst of times all help to create who you are and who you want to be!

3. **Judge less, forgive more, look for the best in all.** Everyone and everything has something positive to offer you. Find it and enlarge your heart and spirit!

4. **Ask, ask, and ask again for what it is you want.** Don't be afraid to ask people for what you want and need. Most people want to help you and will!

5. **Develop a passion for something you want to do.** Take risks and go for more than you think you can. Fear paralyzes and passion is fuel. Believe you can!

6. **Love with all your heart as much as you can.** Take pleasure, play and work seriously, and enjoy yourself. Be grateful for everything all day long!

7. **Live in the moment. Learn from the past. Let the future be designed through your intentions.** You are a master of creation—be open to the process!

Seven Tips for Having Gratitude...

1. **Having gratitude has a cleansing effect** on your mind, body and soul. Noting your blessings enlarges you from within and manifests magic outwardly.

2. **Showing gratitude by saying "Thank You"** all the time for everything, is a wonderful way to increase your awareness for things others take for granted.

3. **Having gratitude allows you to appreciate** your personal wisdom and power, and the gifts the universe is always bringing you through all of life's lessons.

4. **Having gratitude** can alter your energy and make you feel really happy just to be alive, allowing you to experience nothing less than Heaven on earth.

5. **Having gratitude helps you remember** that even in the eye of a storm God has put a rainbow in the clouds. You are blessed and being taken care of.

6. **Having a gratitude attitude changes the world.** A kind thoughtful word goes a long way in opening the hearts, arms and gratitude of others.

7. **Having gratitude can turn your life around.** Just realizing that abundance is truly there for all of us, and being thankful that you are alive is the key.

 *Seven Tips for Making Better Choices...*

1. **Trust your intuition.** Inside each of us is an all-knowing wise self. Trust that you know best. Listen to the voice inside that always guides you.

2. **Create your own value system.** When you live out of your integrity and from your values, you never need to be afraid of making a wrong choice.

3. **Make choices that honor who you are.** When you consciously make choices that will better your life and the people in it, there are only good choices.

4. **Take counsel. Include it all.** All the information, opinions and facts you can get. Then armed with the facts, make your decisions and your best choices.

5. **Welcome it all.** There are no bad choices, just one more way to learn. Everything can be seen in a dozen different ways, it's what you do with it that matters.

6. **Choose the life you want**, not the life you've been told you should live or think you should live. When you choose your deepest desire, magic happens.

7. **Choose to learn to love yourself.** Then choose your life from the strength of knowing your worth, and that you always deserve the best for yourself.

Seven Tips for Not Sabotaging Yourself...

1. **Don't take anything personally.** There is nothing anyone else does because of you, they do it because of themselves and their own insecurities and needs.

2. **Trust your intuition.** Trust that you do know what is the right thing to do. Stop second guessing yourself and trust your own inner wisdom and guidance.

3. **Honor yourself and your uniqueness.** Take care of yourself as you would the most important person. Applaud your accomplishments and acknowledge you.

4. **Don't assume anything.** If you feel like something is wrong and you're feeling uncomfortable, give others a chance to clear it up. Make no assumptions.

5. **Have clear communications.** Ask lots of questions and say what's on your mind. Make sure you understand exactly what's being said or done by others.

6. **Ask for what you want.** Everyone has the right to say yes or no, but you'll never know what they will say if you don't ask! It's just being smart, not pushy.

7. **Be impeccable with your words.** Don't ever use your words against yourself. Use your thoughts and words to empower you, never to disempower.

Seven Tips for Better Acknowledgment Skills...

1. **Practice acknowledging yourself for the courage** it takes to just show up for life, when life seems not to be showing up for you. Bravo brave soul!

2. **Practice acknowledging others for their work.** Everyone is on their own journey and deserves to be acknowledged for all their efforts. Go girl!

3. **Everyday acknowledge something you've done.** Don't waste your time and energy looking for someone else to do it, you know and that's enough!

4. **Acknowledgment is a form of acceptance,** and lack of acknowledgment is a form of judgment. Always voice your approval for yourself and for others.

5. **Acknowledgment is a sign of love;** lack of it says I just don't care. Is that the statement you want to say to yourself or to others? Think about it.

6. **Acknowledge everyone you can, when you can.** Find something worth noting about a friend, loved one, business associate, store helper and strangers.

7. **Acknowledge The Source that created us all.** It's important to remember all the gifts and blessings you've been given, and how good you've turned out.

Seven Tips for Taking Pleasure Seriously...

1. **Pleasure helps us find our genius.** It's usually in the middle of having the best of times that we open ourselves up to our unlimited potential and dreams.

2. **Pleasure is the balancer between work and life.** Without something to take us away from the stress and demands of life, "Jackie becomes a very dull girl."

3. **Pleasure gives us time to idle.** Daydreaming helps us develop new ideas as our problems incubate and creativity flows. So pleasure your way to success!

4. **Pleasurable times help us relax, replenish, and revitalize our human spirit.** It helps us clean out the mental cobwebs and think more clearly.

5. **Pleasure helps to keep enthusiasm up and alive.** When you love what you do, all else will follow. It's the secret elixir to a life filled with joy.

6. **Pleasure is fun and we all need fun in our lives.** Life can be tough and we all need to find ways to rise above life's ups and downs. Take it seriously!

7. **Taking pleasure seriously is an important step** in turning an ordinary life into an *Extraordinary* one. It's the spark that lights the fire within your heart.

Seven Tips for Helping You Relax and Trust...

1. **Seek out solitude.** Go sit in the garden, take a walk, or indulge yourself with a hot soak in the tub. Find alone time to relax and trust into your dreams .

2. **Ask yourself what it is you really want,** not what someone else wants for you. Then relax and trust that the universe will deliver your true intentions.

3. **Tune into yourself.** Exercise your trust muscle by listening to your all-knowing inner voice. All the right answers are waiting within. Relax and Trust.

4. **Forgive yourself** for all the times when you were too afraid or insecure to relax and trust yourself or the universe. Trust and act on your own beliefs.

5. **Learn to enjoy the process.** Everything has a reason for being. Relax and trust that it will all work out fine and eventually it all will.

6. **Live more authentically.** Even if it stir up anxiety and discomfort, it will also give you great joy and power. Trust the process—just relax and trust.

7. **Recognize your own truth, act on that knowledge.** Have the courage to take responsibility for your choices, and then relax and trust into your wisdom.

Seven Tips for Handling Your Fears...

1. **Hope and faith can transform fear.** Use your belief in a higher power to help you move forward. Life can be scary and tough without faith and hope.

2. **Everyone has a certain level of fear.** Dealing with it includes first noticing what pushes your buttons, how you control it, and how you manage it.

3. **Facing fear is a work in progress.** Until you try you'll never know what you can endure or how capable you are in handling problems. Stay strong.

4. **F.E.A.R—false expectations appearing real.** It may be an oldie but goodie, but it's true. You have nothing to fear but fear itself. Think positively.

5. **Fear is often associated with taking a risk,** yet it's often that risk-taking action that frees and moves you away from what you fear the most. Just do it.

6. **Fear often paralyzes you, don't let it.** Do anything that you can to change your environment and your state of mind. Change combats fear.

7. **Remember all the things you have ever feared** that never happened the way you thought they would? Fear is bigger in your mind then in reality.

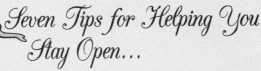

Seven Tips for Helping You Stay Open...

1. **Pay attention and watch.** Since we don't ever know for sure what's really going to happen, stay open and enjoy watching life unfold at your feet.

2. **Life is a jokester, enjoy the joke.** Oftentimes what we think will be wonderful is not and our disappointments become our greatest gift.

3. **Practice good listening techniques.** Listen for more than what is said. Because beyond the words is often the truth of the real message.

4. **Keep your mind open.** Because when your mind is closed you think you know the answer and you are often closing the door to other possibilities.

5. **Magic and miracles are the eternal mysteries of life.** Knowing that you just don't know or even understand is an important step in staying open.

6. **Let go.** The only thing that you know for sure, is that the outcome will look different than your vision—stay open to the essence of what you want.

7. **Don't take life or yourself too seriously.** Everything is temporary and nothing lasts forever. Staying open to everything is the answer.

Seven Tips for Journaling Problems Away...

1. **Journaling first thing in the morning** is a great way to get rid of yesterday's problems and begin the day anew. Begin by just letting the words flow.

2. **Journal just for your eyes only—no one else's.** When you write with the freedom of knowing that no one else will read it—you can tell your truth.

3. **Journal in a safe and comfortable place.** When we feel comfortable and safe we feel free to let our true selves be true to ourselves.

4. **Journal for at least three minutes or more.** Give yourself a fair amount of time to examine your issues and then to express them fully.

5. **Use a pen and pad that you can throw away.** That way you feel no qualms in throwing away your troubles and concerns with it.

6. **Play doctor. Ask the hard questions** and be willing to say what's really on your mind. It's a sure way to get to know the real you.

7. **Journal whenever and wherever** the mood strikes you. If you feel the need, then the need is there. Journal and enjoy the results.

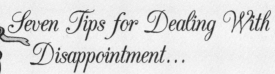

Seven Tips for Dealing With Disappointment...

1. **Make a conscious choice to shed outdated beliefs** that keep you stuck in limited thinking. Open your mind and heart to new ideas and then let it be.

2. **Look at your problem retrospectively,** will this issue really bother you in ten-fifteen years? If the honest answer is no...let it be.

3. **Try deep breathing to center your thoughts.** When you feel caught up in the craziness, count to 10 as you slowly exhale —deep in—slowly out. Let it be.

4. **Practice the art of detachment.** Remember a time in your life when you got what you wanted without being attached to the end result. Let it be.

5. **Find a way to move on** even if things don't work out the way you want. It's a great way to open the door to letting more of what you want come in. Let it be.

6. **Try trusting being yourself.** Once you do, things just seem to fall into place more easily. Almost miraculously you find your answers. Let it be.

7. **Hear the words of wisdom...let it be.** There is no payoff on holding on to upsets or letting it run you for days. It really is wisdom to just let it be.

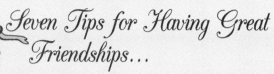

Seven Tips for Having Great Friendships...

1. **True friendships are built on solid foundations.** A true friend will always want to understand how you really feel about everything...no matter what.

2. **Respect for each other is essential in friendships.** Expressing your differences or even disagreements with respect, is a good thing for great friendships.

3. **Sharing your most personal information** with a good friend and knowing that it will be held in the strictest confidence creates great friendships.

4. **Supporting a friend in their time of need,** and being by their side to give them whatever they need—no matter what the circumstances are—that's a friend.

5. **See your friends in their highest light.** When you choose to see the best in your friends, you hold up the mirror for them to reflect their best back to you.

6. **Always listen for the unspoken request.** The words that say, I need or want you in my life now for whatever reason...please say yes and please be there.

7. **Let your friends be there for you.** Everyone wants to be needed so let them. Don't abuse the privilege or be an energy sapper...we all need boundaries.

Seven Tips for Being Frivolous and Decadent...

1. **Don't do anything that feels like responsibility.** The mental benefits of doing things frivolous and decadent, is that it takes you away from drudgery.

2. **Do things that feel childlike.** Kids love doing things that are frivolous and decadent. It makes you feel free, limitless and fill of giggles and joy.

3. **Enjoy little pleasures,** like walking in dewy grass barefoot, eating an ice cream sundae on Monday. Little pleasures can be delicious and naughty!

4. **Enjoy big pleasures,** like going off to a health spa, or parachute jumping, or doing a cooking course in Paris. Just because you can and you deserve it!

5. **Create an at-home-spa.** Pull out the scented everything—candles, oils, incense, perfume, and use them. Then go somewhere else in your mind.

6. **Use your imagination** when you absolutely can't get away. Pretend that you are doing your chores like an actor in a movie—just for the fun of it!

7. **Make your own list** of things that are frivolous and decadent. And one by one, check them off as you do them. Taking care of yourself changes your life!

Seven Tips for Creating Positive Heart Energy...

1. **Find ways to manage your challenges.** Everyone feels down at times, over-whelmed, confused and frustrated. Positive heart energy is a good change.

2. **Confide in those you trust** with your fears, hopes and mistakes. It's one of the best ways to improve your mind-body health, and to create positive energy.

3. **Write it down and then let it go.** Get those nasty feelings out of your body onto paper. It frees up your positive heart energy to create change.

4. **Appreciate and acknowledge others.** Any time you validate, compliment or appreciate another, you create a heartfelt energetic positive effect.

5. **Ask "why not?"** rather than "why." None of us knows for sure what's going to happen, so why not go for it? Positive energy creates courage for risks.

6. **Find the work you were born to do.** When you can actively pursue your passion, your positive change and heartfelt energy creates enthusiasm and joy.

7. **Love it or leave it.** Doing anything and being with anyone that closes your heart is an energy sapper. Positive change and heartfelt energy is where it's at!

Seven Tips for Enhancing Your Self-Respect...

1. **You teach others how to treat you.** It's up to you to show others what is acceptable to you, what your standards and boundaries are. What you need.

2. **Don't expect more than you're willing to give.** Don't expect to get without having to give in return. Show respect for others and others will respect you.

3. **Love yourself first.** Relationships mirror each other's actions and reactions. You can only receive as much respect as you are willing to give yourself.

4. **Know thine own self.** Know what it is that you really want and need. Ask for it without apologies or manipulating others. Listen to what others need.

5. **Take care of your own needs first.** Others want to give you more when it's their choice to give you what you want, not just because you are needy.

6. **Find out and give others what they need,** not what you want or think they need. Give to others as you would want others to give to you in return.

7. **Don't sell yourself short or play small.** There is no benefit to anyone when you diminish your self-respect or needs. Stand tall and play full out.

Seven Tips for Increasing Your Self-Worth...

1. **Make a promise to always be true to yourself.** When you honor your own wishes and needs first, then you never have to feel used or abused.

2. **Recognize your uniqueness.** Never forget that there is no one like you, so honor your differences. You are a rare and special jewel. Treasure that.

3. **Always express yourself in the way you want to.** Your opinions matters and your style is your own. Your ways are special to you and worth expressing.

4. **Learn how to support yourself.** Give yourself the gift of faith, courage and the confidence to be who you are and who you want to be...you're worth it!

5. **Learn to see yourself clearly,** through your own honest loving eyes. You can't be all things to all people, so find out who you are and then be true to it.

6. **Know your worth and value.** Never judge yourself by someone else's standards or expectations. Your personal worth is what you determine it to be.

7. **Honor who you are** rather than what others have defined you as. Let go of the outdated need to please others to be accepted—you already are the best!

Seven Tips for Enhancing Self-Esteem...

1. **Do it anyway! Take risks! Let yourself feel success!** No one can make you feel worthy or successful but you. Do whatever you need to do to feel that way.

2. **The best you can do is notice what's happening.** It's ok to feel anxious, scared or lazy. As long as you don't let that stop you from moving forward.

3. **You need to have a purpose.** You need to know where you want to be, and what you need to get there. The process keeps you moving to who you want to be.

4. **Self-esteem takes introspection and comparisons.** Find your unique ways of being one of a kind. Compare your assets—learn to love and honor your gifts.

5. **Make a list of things that make you feel proud** of yourself. Make that list once a week. When you doubt your worth, bring out the list and read it.

6. **Discover you. Get to know the you worth loving.** Self-esteem comes from having great esteem for who you are, what you do and why you're special.

7. **Learn to accept the things that you can't change.** If it's your body, remember how it has served you. If you think you're not enough. Know that's a lie!

Seven Tips for Kindness That Changes Things...

1. **Take a minute and listen to what others say.** Oftentimes all anyone wants is to be listened to. Taking the time to listen can change everything.

2. **Do something totally thoughtful** and totally unexpected. Doing a random act of kindness can fill up a heart and soul like nothing else can.

3. **Be kind to your supposed enemies.** Nothing can change a negative situation into a positive one like love and sincere kindness.

4. **Treat the little people like the big people.** When you get into the habit op treating everyone the same, everyone feels equally good.

5. **Kindness is a way of life and an attitude.** It's true; what you put out you get back. If kindness is your way of life, life will be kind to you.

6. **Be as kind to yourself as you are to others.** Never forget that kindness starts at home. Spend today being kind to yourself.

7. **Random acts of kindness,** without a concern as to whether or not you are acknowledged for them, builds personal worth, value and self-esteem.

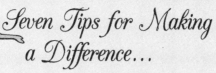

Seven Tips for Making a Difference...

1. **Always remember, it's quality not quantity.** If your actions are generated from a loving heart, just a few words at the right time can make a difference.

2. **Compassion is what people need more than anything.** Really listening to someone's problems and concerns, can be all that they need to know someone cares.

3. **Go that extra mile when someone is in need.** By taking the time to call, write, email or go visit, just your efforts can be enough to make a difference.

4. **Show others who they really are.** When you can be a mirror reflection of another's perfection, you give them the opportunity to see their best side.

5. **Speak to someone's higher self,** instead of their past performances or historical behavior. Give others the chance to do better or even change.

6. **Keep a secret.** When people know that they can tell you something really private and it won't go any further, it frees them up to tell their truth.

7. **You can make a difference** when you give up how it looks to others, or how important what you are doing is. Care about others and you can change the world.

Seven Tips for Joy to Be Your Peak Experience...

1. **Make JOY a priority in your life.** Look for anything and everything that can bring you happiness and JOY. If you're not joyful, change what you're doing.

2. **Never confuse a lack of JOY** with lack of money, what you have or don't have, or who you are. JOY is always within you and always within your reach.

3. **JOY is the most direct connection,** in the deepest way, to your spiritual self. It strengthen your sense of appreciation and gratitude for all of life.

4. **Become aware that JOY is always a choice.** In every moment you have the opportunity to choose JOY as your highest commitment—your way of life.

5. **JOY and love go hand and hand.** Find the piece in everyone and everything that you can love and enjoy. Learn to joyfully love it all, now and forever.

6. **When you use JOY as your source of strength,** and inspiration, you experience more love, happiness, prosperity, contentment and peace in your life.

7. **Say yes to JOY.** A yes that makes the earth shake and the walls tremble. Scream "yes" to it all! Yes, I am ready for a life of technicolor JOY!